Break Through!

The Bible for Young Catholics

Old Testament
Activity Booklet

saint mary's press

The activity pages were created and designed by Gabriel Publications. The background pages were created from content supplied by Therese Brown, Rick Keller-Scholz, Christine Schmertz Navarro, Ann Nunes, Jeannie Pomanowski, Brian Singer-Towns, and Chris Wardwell.

The publishing team included Gloria Shahin, editorial director; and Joanna Dailey, editor. Prepress and manufacturing coordinated by the production departments of Saint Mary's Press.

The bookshelf illustration on page 8 is by Paul Casper; all other illustrations are by Pernsteiner Creative Group.

Printed in the United States of America

4351

ISBN 978-1-59982-221-1

Contents

Student Introduction

You may not have thought of this, but the people in the Old Testament are part of your family. That is because you and they are all part of the family of God. The people of the Old Testament have a special place in our family. Through their stories we learn in a unique way about God and about how God wants us to live. Each person of the Old Testament has something important to teach us if we take the time to learn his or her story.

You may think every person in the Old Testament lived a perfect life. Not so! As you go through the pages in this activity booklet, you will learn about eleven brothers who sold their youngest brother into slavery. You will learn about a warrior leader who kept chasing foreign women. You will learn about a king who taxed his people too much and divided the kingdom. Sometimes we learn from an Old Testament person's good examples, and sometimes we learn from her or his mistakes. But the most important thing you will learn is that God never abandoned them if they were sorry and returned to God.

You may also think: "These people are ancient! What do they have to do with my life?" You may be surprised at the familiar issues Old Testament people dealt with. Many had family rivalries with brothers or sisters. Some wrestled with feelings of jealousy or insecurity. Others doubted God's call, yet continued the conversation until God convinced them!

The booklet begins with five activity pages that will help you learn a little bit about all the books of the Bible, how the Bible is organized, and a little bit about Bible history. Then there are activity pages for thirty-four different Old Testament people. (You will find activities for New Testament people in *Breakthrough! The Bible for Young Catholics: New Testament Activity Booklet.*) The activity pages are kind of like puzzles. To do the puzzles, you will need to follow the activity's directions. Usually you will need to look up some Bible passages to finish the activity.

On the back of each activity page is a background page with information on the Old Testament person or topic. This page usually contains a short description of the person, Bible passages and *Breakthrough!* articles about that person, and some reflection questions. If you are using this booklet in a school or parish, your teacher or catechist will give you directions about how and when to use a background page.

This booklet is best used with *Breakthrough! The Bible for Young Catholics. Breakthrough!* was created for young people like you. It has many special features that help to make the Bible easier to read and understand.

Teacher, Catechist, Parent Introduction

You can use *Breakthrough! The Bible for Young Catholics: Old Testament Activity Booklet* in several ways to teach in your school, parish, or home.

Introducing Basic Biblical Literacy

The first five activities introduce the young people to some basic concepts of biblical literacy. The first activity has them use the table of contents to become familiar with the names of biblical books. The second and third activities help the young people become familiar with the Old and New Testaments. The fourth activity begins to help them see the connections between the Old and New Testaments. The fifth activity is intended to be used as an introduction to the big picture of salvation history.

You will note that this *Old Testament Activity Booklet* includes an introduction to both the Old and New Testaments. While studying the Old Testament, it is important to realize its integral connection to the New Testament. God's Revelation in the Old Testament prepares us for his complete Revelation in the New Testament, in Jesus Christ.

Depending on your situation, you can use these activity pages in different ways. You can use all five activities before your study of Old Testament people. Or you may wish to use "Introduction to the Old Testament" before studying Old Testament people and reserve using the activity pages for "Introduction to the New Testament" for your study of the New Testament in the *Breakthrough! New Testament Activity Booklet*, where these pages also appear. You might summarize your study of the Old and New Testaments with the "Connections" and "Salvation History" activities. They are yours to use in whatever way is most appropriate.

Learning about the Bible People

There are three easy ways that students can learn about a biblical person on their own: First, they can read the brief description from the background page about that person. Second, they can look up and read as many as six biblical passages, listed on the background page, that relate to that biblical person, and they can read listed articles from *Breakthrough!* Third, to see if they have retained the main elements of the biblical person's story, students can complete the biblical person's activity page.

Going Deeper into a Character Study

If the students have already become acquainted with the biblical person's story, they will be ready to look at the character in greater depth with you. You may use the reflection questions at the bottom of the background page either by themselves or in conjunction with the *Breakthrough! Old Testament Leader Guide*. The majority of the reflection questions in the activity booklet are inspired by the longer activities in the leader guide.

The students should initially answer the reflection questions privately and in writing. Depending on the question, you may want to invite the young people to share something they wrote or any thoughts that came to them because of the questions. Although a question may ask them something personal, all questions relate back to the biblical person.

Reviewing

If you teach about a character starting with the longer activities in the *Breakthrough! Old Testament Leader Guide,* these activity pages can be helpful for review. If the students seem to be struggling with certain parts of the activity, you can review those parts of the biblical person's story that are causing them trouble.

The Short Stop

If you have limited time, these activities can enable you to quickly cover some characters that are less known or overlooked. Though you may want to spend more time with Isaiah than with Ezekiel, the students can still get to know Ezekiel from his activity page and background page in this activity booklet.

The Answers

The correct answers for all the activities in this booklet can be found in appendix 3 of the *Breakthrough! Old Testament Leader Guide*. It is always a good idea to complete an activity page yourself before assigning it to the young people. This way you can gauge its difficulty and appropriateness. The booklet pages are perforated to make them easy to collect for review or grading.

Bible Books

Read the list of the names of the books in the table of contents of your Bible. Hidden in each of the sentences below is the name of one of those books. For example, in the sentence "I ran because I was afraid the snake was going to bite me," the Book of TOBIT is hidden (. . . was going **TO BIT**e me.) Find the book name hidden in each of these sentences and write it on the line provided.

1. While they were playing outside, Jim took a hose and sprayed his sister.

   _____

2. Jennifer cannot go to the beach with us because she has a job for the summer.

   _____

3. When the customer asked the mechanic if he could fix the car, he replied, "Sir, a child could do it."

   _____

4. When we rode in the parade in a Cadillac sedan, I elevated the convertible roof.

   _____

5. As soon as I looked up, I saw Sam at the window waving to me.

   _____

6. John Fitzgerald Kennedy was the first Catholic president of the United States.

   _____

7. The jury knew the man was guilty from answers he gave when he testified at the trial.

   _____

8. We learned about number sets in Mrs. Jones's math class today.

   _____

9. I gave Andrea most of the candy I bought at the store.

   _____

10. I like strawberry jam, especially when I have it on toast for breakfast.

    _____

Bible Books

The Bible is not really one book; it is a collection of books. There are seventy-three books in Catholic Bibles: forty-six books in the Old Testament and twenty-seven books in the New Testament. The books are not all the same kind of writing. Some books are poetry, some are letters, some are short stories, and some are reflections on how God was working though historical people and events.

The books are divided into two major sections, the Old Testament and the New Testament. The Old Testament books are primarily about God's special relationship with his Chosen People. At different times these people are called Hebrews, Israelites, Judeans, and Jews. The New Testament books are about God's biggest breakthrough in history: the coming of Jesus Christ. The New Testament stories tell about Jesus' life and mission, starting with God's Chosen People, the Jews. The New Testament books tell how Jesus' first disciples quickly expanded the mission to include non-Jews, called Gentiles.

The Old Testament and the New Testament are further divided into other sections, shown in the diagram below. You can find more information on those sections in the background pages for the next two activities.

Finding Bible Passages

The Bible has a system for helping you locate specific passages. Each book in the Bible is divided into chapters (except for some very short books). The chapter numbers are the larger ones on the page. Each chapter is divided into verses. A verse is usually about a sentence long. The verse numbers are the smaller numbers in each chapter and start with verse 1 in each new chapter.

A Bible citation is a code for finding a passage using this system. A citation has three parts: the Bible book name, a chapter number, and verse numbers. So John 3:16–17 means the Gospel of John, chapter three, verse sixteen through verse seventeen.

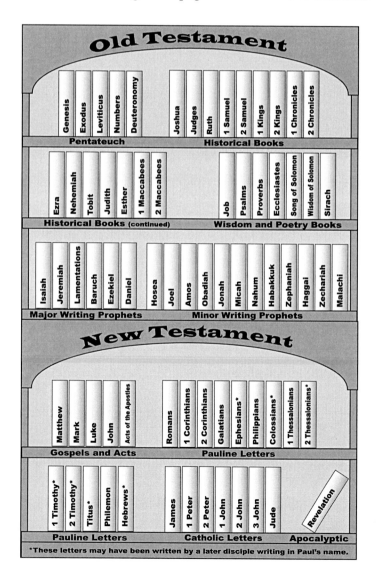

Introduction to the Old Testament

Turn to the table of contents in the beginning of your Bible and use it to answer the following questions about the Old Testament.

1. How many books are in the Old Testament? _____

2. What is the first book of the Old Testament? _____

3. What is the last book of the Old Testament? _____

4. Which book of the Old Testament is the shortest? _____

5. Which book of the Old Testament is the longest? _____

6. What are the four sections of the Old Testament? _____

_____

_____

_____

7. List the five books of the Pentateuch. _____

_____

_____

_____

_____

8. Which book comes after Psalms? _____

9. In which section do you find each of the following books?

1 Kings _____   Nahum _____

Song of Songs _____   Jonah _____

Now try looking up some Bible passages. Look up each passage below and write the word indicated to complete a sentence about the Old Testament.

10. **Exodus 12:37**   Write the second word of the passage in the space before the (10).

11. **Judges 10:14**   Write the tenth word of the passage in the space before the (11).

12. **Isaiah 32:18**   Write the second word of the passage in the space before the (12).

The Old Testament is the story of the _____ (10),

God's _____ (11) _____ (12).

Introduction to the Old Testament

The Old Testament in Catholic Bibles contains forty-six books. The Bibles that most Protestants use has thirty-nine books in the Old Testament. That is the main difference between Catholic and Protestant Bibles.

The Old Testament books include many different kinds of writings. You will find history, poetry, legends, laws, wise sayings, short stories, and the words of prophets. The Old Testament books are primarily about God's special relationship with his Chosen People. At different times these people are called Hebrews, Israelites, Judeans, and Jews. During their history God breaks through and calls the Chosen People to recognize him as their one and only God. God promises to bless them in a special way, and he asks the Chosen People to be faithful in following his commands.

This holy promise between God and the Chosen People is called a covenant. *Testament* is another word for *covenant,* so the Old Testament is the story of the covenant between God and his special people—who eventually become the Jewish people. Because of this, most of the books of the Old Testament are also the sacred Scriptures of the Jewish people, sometimes called the Hebrew Scriptures.

To fully understand God's plan for the human race, we need both the Old and the New Testaments. In the Old Testament, God reveals the love he has for us. The stories teach us how sin keeps us from being in a completely loving relationship with God. The Old Testament shows how, through various people, God broke through to put his Chosen People on the right path.

REFLECTION

1. Page through the Old Testament of your Bible. What stories do you recognize? If you have any favorite stories in the Old Testament, what are they? What do they teach you about God?

2. Flip through the interview pages of the Old Testament Bible people (Adam and Eve through Lady Wisdom) in *Breakthrough! The Bible for Young Catholics.* Which Old Testament Bible people are you most curious about? Why?

Sections of the Old Testament

The Old Testament in Christian Bibles is usually divided into four different sections. Here's some information on each section:

The Pentateuch or Torah These five books are the heart of the Old Testament. They contain the stories of Creation and stories about how sin entered the world. They tell how God broke through to first make his covenant with Noah and Abraham. The Book of Exodus tells how God led his people out of slavery through the leadership of Moses. At Mount Sinai, God extended the covenant to all his Chosen People and gave them the Ten Commandments.

The Historical Books These sixteen books are mostly religious history and some short novels. They tell how the Chosen People settled in the Promised Land. Eventually they became a kingdom led by kings like Saul, David, and Solomon. But the rulers and the people often worshipped false gods and ignored the poor. So God sent prophets like Elijah and Elisha to call the people to be faithful to the covenant. The historical books have imaginative stories about heroes like Ruth, Tobit, Judith, and Esther.

The Wisdom Books These seven books contain the collected wisdom of the Chosen People. They contain the songs they used in worship and prayer. They contain advice for living a good and holy life. The Song of Songs has poetry about the goodness of sexuality. The Book of Job is a debate about why good people suffer bad things.

The Books of the Prophets These eighteen books contain the messages of important prophets. The prophets delivered God's message to the Chosen People. They warned the Chosen People against worshipping false gods. They challenged the Chosen People to act fairly and to care for the poor. The prophets also offered comfort and hope when the people thought God had abandoned them. And some of the prophets promised a future savior, the Messiah, who would bring God's love, justice, and peace to the world.

Name: _____

Introduction to the New Testament

Turn to the table of contents in the beginning of your Bible and use it and the books of the New Testament to answer the following questions on the New Testament.

1. How many books are in the New Testament? _____

2. What is the first book of the New Testament? _____

3. What is the last book of the New Testament? _____

4. Which book in the New Testament is the longest? _____

5. Which book in the New Testament is the shortest? _____

6. List the four Gospels. _____

_____

_____

_____

7. List at least three letters (Epistles). _____

_____

_____

8. What book comes right after the Gospel of John? _____

Now try looking up some Bible passages. Look up each passage below and write the word indicated to complete a sentence about the New Testament.

9. **Matthew 4:7**   Write the first word of the passage in the space before the (9).

10. **Romans 8:10**   Write the third word of the passage in the space before the (10).

11. **Mark 14:12**   Write the third word of the passage in the space before the (11).

12. **Acts 11:26**   Write the last word of the passage in the space before the (12).

The New Testament tells us about _____(9) _____(10)

and the _____(11) _____(12).

Introduction to the New Testament

The New Testament contains twenty-seven books. These books contain several kinds of writings. You will find Gospels, religious history, letters to individuals, letters to communities, homilies, and visions. All these books are in some way about God's biggest breakthrough in history: the coming of Jesus Christ. The New Testament stories tell how Jesus' mission starts with God's Chosen People, whom today we call the Jews. They also tell how Jesus' first disciples quickly expanded the mission to include non-Jews, who were called Gentiles.

Testament is another word for *covenant,* and a covenant is a holy promise made between God and human beings. The Old Testament is about the original covenant that God made with his Chosen People. The New Testament writings show how the promises of the covenant in the Old Testament were fulfilled by Jesus Christ. Through Jesus, God extended the covenant to the whole human race. We call this the New Covenant, the promise that every person—Jew or Gentile—can have eternal life with God. This New Testament tells how this was made possible by Jesus' life, death, and Resurrection. To fully understand God's plan for the human race, we need both the Old and the New Testaments.

REFLECTION

1. Page through the New Testament of your Bible. What stories do you recognize? If you have any favorite stories in the New Testament, what are they? What do they teach you about Jesus Christ?

2. Flip through the interview pages of the New Testament Bible people (Mary of Nazareth to Priscilla and Aquila) in *Breakthrough! The Bible for Young Catholics.* Which New Testament Bible people are you most curious about? Why?

Sections of the New Testament

The New Testament is usually divided into two or three main sections. Here's some information on each section:

The Gospels and the Acts of the Apostles
Gospel literally means "good news." We call Matthew, Mark, Luke, and John Gospels because they tell the Good News of Jesus Christ. These four books each have their unique picture of Jesus Christ. It is believed that Mark was written first. The writers of Matthew and Luke probably used Mark as a starting point in creating their Gospels. That is why these three Gospels have some very similar stories.

The Gospel of John is quite different from the other three. There are fewer miracles and fewer parables, and John more clearly presents Jesus as God's Son. Having four Gospels gives us a more complete understanding of Jesus than having just one.

The Acts of the Apostles picks up where the Gospels leave off. Acts tells the exciting story of the first Christians. By traveling and preaching, they spread the Good News of Jesus Christ throughout the known world.

The Letters At the time of Jesus, there was no telephone, television, radio, or Internet. So when the early leaders of the Church wanted to communicate, they did so by writing letters. These letters were written to groups and to individuals. They helped the first Christians—and they help us—understand what it means to be a follower of Jesus.

The majority of the letters were written by Saint Paul or by people writing in his name. It was not uncommon at that time to honor a great person by writing letters or books in his or her name.

Revelation The Revelation to John is not a letter but a collection of prophecies and visions. It is about the struggle between the good and evil forces that exist in the world. Revelation promises that even though believers will be persecuted, God will make everything right in the end.

Connections

In this activity you will match an Old Testament passage about the Messiah to a New Testament passage about the life of Jesus. In each box there is an Old Testament passage for you to read and some space for you to write down a few key words from the passage.

After you have read the passages in the boxes, read the passages listed at the bottom of the page. Match each of these New Testament passages to one of the Old Testament passages in the boxes. The Old Testament passage is either quoted in the New Testament passage or describes a person or event from the New Testament passage. Write in the appropriate box the number of the New Testament passage. When you finish, the numbers you have put in the boxes should add up to the same total across, up and down, and diagonally.

OLD TESTAMENT PASSAGES		
Isaiah 61:1–2	Malachi 3:1–3	Isaiah 9:1–2
Micah 5:2	Isaiah 35:5–6	Genesis 12:1–3
Jeremiah 31:31–34	Isaiah 7:14	Zechariah 9:9

NEW TESTAMENT PASSAGES

1. Matthew 1:23
2. Luke 4:16–19
3. Matthew 1:1
4. Matthew 4:12–16
5. Matthew 11:3–6
6. Luke 22:20
7. Luke 2:4–7
8. Matthew 21:1–11
9. John 2:13–17

Connections

Different people, in different places, in different times wrote the books of the Bible. Because of this, you might think that there would be hardly any connections among the Bible's books. But the opposite is true; there are many connections among the different books of the Bible. This is partly because the authors of later books were familiar with the books that were already written. The Holy Spirit also guided the authors of the Bible's books in making connections between the life of Jesus and the Old Testament people and stories.

Here are some of the kinds of connections you will find among the books of the Bible:

- Sometimes several books told stories about the same people or events. Think of the four Gospels—Matthew, Mark, Luke, and John—which are all slightly different versions of the things Jesus said and did.
- Sometimes people in one book say things that are from a different book. For example, when Jesus says, "Love the Lord your God with all your heart, with all your soul, and with all your mind" (Matthew 22:37), he is quoting Deuteronomy 6:5.
- As Christians, we see in some Old Testament passages signs of events that happened in Jesus' life. As an example, the Suffering Servant passages (Isaiah 42:1–7, 49:1–6, 50:4–9, 52:13—53:12) point to Jesus' own suffering and death.

To fully understand God's message in the Bible, it helps to understand these connections. They show how God has been breaking through all human history with his message of love. The stories of the Old Testament are part of the complete story of God's plan of salvation history that reaches its fulfillment in the coming of Jesus Christ, which is told in the New Testament. The connections between the Old and New Testaments and among other parts of the Bible show how God has been at work for thousands of years, trying to break through to us with his message of love.

REFLECTION

1. Which person from the Old Testament most reminds you of Jesus? Why?

2. Think about Bible stories that have a connection to water, such as the story about Jonah and the giant fish. Make a list of all the stories you can think of. Many of these stories have a connection to the Sacrament of Baptism. What do the stories you thought of teach us about Baptism?

Breakthrough! Articles

Read these articles to learn more about some of the connections in the Bible.

Salvation History

History told from the perspective of God's breaking through is called salvation history. Look at the time line in the front of *Breakthrough!* This time line gives a big-picture view of salvation history. In the boxes below, create your own big picture of salvation history by drawing an event that occurred during each time period. Write a brief caption for each drawing.

PRIMEVAL HISTORY CREATION–2000 BC	PATRIARCHS 2000 BC–1700 BC
EGYPT AND THE EXODUS 1700 BC–1250 BC	**SETTLING THE PROMISED LAND** 1250 BC–1050 BC
KINGDOMS OF JUDAH AND ISRAEL 1050 BC–587 BC	**EXILE AND RETURN** 587 BC–AD 1
LIFE OF JESUS CHRIST AD 1–AD 33	**EARLY CHRISTIAN CHURCH** AD 33–AD 100

Salvation History

The Bible tells the story of how God breaks through to save human beings from sin and bring us to eternal life—also called salvation history. Here's a brief description of eight periods of salvation history.

Primeval history The Bible begins with imaginative stories about how God created everything that exists. The stories of Adam and Eve, Cain and Abel, Noah and the Flood, and the tower of Babel teach us that God created everything and that human beings have a special place in creation. They teach us that sin destroys our relationships with God and one another.

Patriarchs In this period of salvation history, God begins to form a special relationship with a chosen race of people. He makes a special promise, called a covenant, with a man named Abraham and his wife, Sarah. God promises that their descendants will be numerous and that they will inherit a Promised Land.

Egypt and the Exodus The descendants of Abraham—now called Israelites—are in slavery in Egypt. God hears their cries, and calls Moses to lead the people out of slavery. The Israelites' escape from Egypt and journey to the Holy Land is called the Exodus. On the way to the Promised Land, the Israelites stop at Mount Sinai. There, God gives Moses the Ten Commandments, which the people must obey as part of their covenant promises.

Settling the Promised Land Moses dies, and God calls a new leader, Joshua, to lead the people into the Promised Land, which is inhabited by other people. The Israelites must fight to gain control. When they trust God, they are successful in their battles; when they do not trust God, they fail. Eventually they gain control of the land, and each of the Twelve Tribes is given their own section of the land.

Kingdoms of Judah and Israel When the Israelites want their own king, God reluctantly answers their plea. He has Samuel anoint Saul as the first king of Israel. David follows Saul as the next king. David unites all the Twelve Tribes into one kingdom. After Solomon's death there is disagreement between the tribes, and the kingdom splits in two: Israel and Judah. During this time God calls prophets to call the people to obey their covenant with God.

Exile and return Despite the prophets' warnings, the people of Israel and Judah continue to turn away from God's covenant with them. So God lets their kingdoms be conquered. Many of the people are taken into captivity, so this period is called the Exile. Fifty years later a new king allows the people—now called Judeans or Jews—to return to rebuild Jerusalem and the Temple.

Life of Jesus Christ When the time is right, God sends his only Son, Jesus Christ, into the world. When Jesus was born, the Romans ruled Israel. Some of the Jews were hoping for a mighty warrior and king like David, who would drive the Romans out. Instead, Jesus preaches love, justice, and forgiveness. When Jesus is killed, his followers think all is lost. Instead, after three days God raises Jesus from the dead!

Early Christian Church After his Resurrection, Jesus instructs his closest followers, the Apostles, to go and spread the Good News of salvation to all people. The Holy Spirit gives the Apostles the courage to tell others about Jesus Christ. Sometimes the Apostles are persecuted by people who do not believe in Jesus. Soon Christianity spread throughout the whole Roman Empire.

Bible People in Salvation History

Primeval History
- Adam and Eve
- Noah

Patriarchs
- Abraham and Sarah
- Jacob, Leah, and Rachel
- Joseph and his brothers

Egypt and the Exodus
- Moses
- Miriam and Aaron

Settling the Promised Land
- Joshua
- Deborah
- Gideon
- Samson
- Ruth

Kingdoms of Judah and Israel
- Samuel
- King Saul
- King David
- King Solomon
- King Hezekiah
- King Josiah
- Elijah and Elisha
- Amos
- Hosea
- Isaiah
- Jeremiah

Exile and Return
- Ezekiel
- Ezra and Nehemiah
- Esther
- The Maccabees

Life of Jesus Christ
- Jesus of Nazareth, the Christ
- Mary of Nazareth
- John the Baptist
- Peter
- Mary Magdalene

Early Christian Church
- Peter
- Paul
- Barnabas
- Timothy
- Priscilla and Aquila

Name: _____

Adam and Eve

Read the story of Adam and Eve in Genesis 2:4—3:24, then fill in the blanks in the statements below. To find out if your answers are correct, find each one in the word search. Write the unused letters from the word search in the spaces at the bottom of the page to spell out a fact about Adam and Eve.

1. When the Lord God created the earth, nothing was growing on it because there was no __ __ __ __ and no man to cultivate the ground.

2. The Lord God formed man out of the clay, or soil, of the __ __ __ __ __ __ .

3. The Lord God planted a garden in __ __ __ __ .

4. The tree of __ __ __ __ was planted in the middle of the garden.

5. There was a stream, or river, in the garden that divided into __ __ __ __ branches.

6. The job of the __ __ __ was to cultivate and care for the garden.

7. The man was allowed to eat of any tree except the tree of the knowledge of __ __ __ __ and bad.

8. The man gave names to all the __ __ __ __ __ __ __ .

9. The woman was made from one of the __ __ __ __ of the man.

10. The snake tempted the woman to eat the __ __ __ __ __ .

11. The man and the woman realized that they were naked and sewed together some __ __ __ __ __ __ __ __ . (TWO WORDS)

12. They hid among some __ __ __ __ __ when they heard the Lord God in the garden.

13. The man named his wife Eve because she was the __ __ __ __ __ __ of all human beings.

14. The __ __ __ __ __ __ __ made clothes from animal skins for them. (TWO WORDS)

15. The Lord God sent the man and the woman out of the garden and placed a flaming __ __ __ __ __ outside it to guard the tree of life.

A	D	A	L	O	R	D	G	O	D
A	D	N	M	A	F	R	N	D	G
D	R	I	E	V	I	E	D	O	N
N	O	M	S	B	G	I	O	I	E
U	W	A	S	E	L	D	A	R	F
O	S	L	S	O	E	R	B	U	I
R	E	S	Y	E	A	R	D	O	L
G	N	E	D	E	V	G	T	F	M
O	M	O	T	H	E	R	D	+	A
T	I	U	R	F	S	+	+	+	N

__ __ __ __   __ __ __   __ __ __

__ __ __ __ __ __ __ __ __

__ __ __.

Adam and Eve

The story of Adam and Eve, the first humans, reveals some basic truths about what it means to be human.

In the story from the Book of Genesis, God creates Adam, whose name means "human being," by forming him from the earth and breathing life into him. Then God creates a woman from Adam's flesh so that Adam will have a companion just like him. The woman's name, Eve, means "living." God puts Adam and Eve in the wonderful Garden of Eden, where they live in peaceful friendship with God, each other, and all of creation. In the garden, they have everything they need to be happy.

Unfortunately, a tricky snake persuades them that what God has given them is not enough. He says that if they eat the fruit of a tree that God has forbidden, they will become just like God. Rather than trusting God, they listen to the snake and eat the forbidden fruit.

This first disobedience is called Original Sin, and it caused Adam and Eve—and every person after them except Jesus and his mother, Mary—to be separated from God, one another, and the rest of creation. Although human beings continued to disobey God, God did not abandon them. Instead, he overcame the damage of Original Sin through the saving work of his Son, Jesus.

REFLECTION

Answer these questions after you have read about Adam and Eve.

1. Imagine you could put Adam, Eve, and the serpent on trial in a courtroom. Who would be most guilty in the case of the first sin? Who would be least guilty? Do any of these characters deserve the most blame? Why or why not?

2. Adam and Eve did not know they were naked until they sinned. Their sin made them ashamed of themselves, and they wanted to cover up. How do people today try to "cover up" the bad feelings they have when they sin? Why do you think people have those feelings of shame after they sin?

Bible Passages about Adam and Eve

Genesis 2:4–15
God creates a man, animals, and a woman.

Genesis 3:1–6
Adam and Eve eat from the forbidden fruit tree.

Genesis 3:7–13
Adam and Eve hide from God.

Genesis 3:14–24
God punishes and banishes Adam and Eve.

Breakthrough! Articles

Read these articles to learn more about Adam and Eve.

Breakthrough! **Interview with Adam and Eve**

Uncovering the Truth
Genesis 2:5–25

Original Sin
Genesis 3:1–24

Noah

The story of Noah is the story of a new creation. In the sixth chapter of Genesis, the very book that told of God's creation of the world and of Adam and Eve, we find that the people God created have disappointed him—everyone except Noah. God chooses Noah as the beginning of a new creation, a second chance for the human race.

The story of Noah and his boat, or ark, is outlined in the puzzle below. Fill in the blanks with the correct answers. Then find your answers in the word search. Two extra words in the word search will tell you something more about the story of Noah. Write them in the sentence at the bottom of the page.

1. Noah had a wife and three sons: Shem, Ham, and ___ ___ ___ ___ ___ ___ ___.

2. God decided to destroy human beings because the world was full of their ___ ___ ___ ___ ___ ___ ___ deeds.

3. God directed Noah to build a ___ ___ ___ ___.

4. Noah took his ___ ___ ___ ___, his sons and their ___ ___ ___ ___ ___, and a male and a ___ ___ ___ ___ ___ ___ of every kind of animal and bird with him into the ark.

5. Rain fell on the earth for ___ ___ ___ ___ ___ days and ___ ___ ___ ___ ___ nights.

6. After the rain stopped, Noah opened a window. First he sent out a ___ ___ ___ ___ ___. It did not come back.

7. Then Noah sent out a ___ ___ ___ ___. It flew back to Noah.

8. Seven days later, he sent out the same bird. It returned to him with an ___ ___ ___ ___ ___ branch in its beak. Noah knew that the waters had gone down.

9. Seven days later he sent out the same bird. This time it did not ___ ___ ___ ___ ___ ___.

10. God blessed Noah and his sons and made a ___ ___ ___ ___ ___ ___ ___ ___ with Noah.

11. God said that he would never ___ ___ ___ ___ ___ ___ ___ the world again by flood.

12. As a sign of this promise, God set a ___ ___ ___ ___ ___ ___ ___ in the sky.

D	F	H	M	N	E	N	R	Z	F	S	M
L	O	C	T	A	O	B	W	E	F	F	M
F	R	R	L	O	U	I	M	Q	V	N	L
O	T	U	J	R	L	A	W	I	V	E	S
R	Y	H	N	A	L	I	O	A	T	L	R
T	A	C	S	E	P	L	V	N	N	D	A
Y	K	V	U	Q	E	H	A	E	E	R	I
U	R	N	E	N	O	N	E	S	E	T	N
W	A	L	T	N	E	C	T	T	E	H	B
I	U	R	S	V	V	R	U	J	H	R	O
F	M	V	O	A	O	R	K	X	Y	J	W
E	S	C	P	Y	N	E	P	D	O	V	E

The ___ ___ ___ (sailing vessel) is a symbol of the ___ ___ ___ ___ ___ ___ (People of God).

Noah

What do we learn about God from the story of Noah? The story of Noah teaches us that God is both just and merciful. God is just, and he cannot be fooled. He knows what is going on with the people he has created, including us! In the story of Noah, those people who chose violence and evil as a way of life were punished by death. However, Noah and his family, who persisted in living good lives, were rewarded with life.

The story of Noah is a picture of what happens in our lives. Does this mean that if we choose a violent and evil way of life, we will end up drowning in a flood? No. But gradually we will lose our true identities as loving human beings, made in the image and likeness of God. We will distort God's good creation of us and become something he never intended us to be. We will lose God's life within us.

The story of Noah reminds us that God is also merciful. Our God is a God of second chances. Even if we have made wrong choices, we can repent. We can turn back to God. In time God sent his only Son, Jesus Christ, to assure us of God's forgiveness and, ultimately, life forever with him.

REFLECTION

Answer these questions after you have read about Noah.

1. Read about God's covenant with Noah in Genesis 9:8–17. This covenant is called the Noahic Covenant. Think of this covenant the next time you see a rainbow! Why do you think God included the birds and animals in this covenant? What does this say about our connection as human beings to the other creatures that God has made? What is our responsibility toward the earth and all of its creatures?

2. Imagine yourself as one of Noah's family. You have just heard God's promise of an everlasting covenant. After being saved in the ark, what is your response to God? What promise do you make to God as part of your participation in this covenant? Write it here.

Bible Passages about Noah

Genesis 6:9–22
God asks Noah to build an ark.

Genesis 7:6–16
Noah, his family, and the animals enter the ark.

Genesis 8:1–12
The flood ends.

Genesis 9:1–17
God makes a covenant with Noah.

Breakthrough! Articles

Read these articles to learn more about Noah.

Finding Hope
Genesis 6:1–12

Got Gratitude?
Genesis 8:20–22

A Promising Sign
Genesis 9:8–17

Name: _____

Abraham

Put the events of Abraham's life in the correct order. You can figure this out by scanning the headlines in Genesis 11:27—23:20. Number the events, 1 through 14, in the space provided. Starting with event number 1, write the bold, underlined letters in the spaces provided at the bottom. Some events have two letters in bold, underlined type. Be sure to write those letters in the spaces in the order in which they appear in the sentence.

1. _____ Hagar gave birth to A**b**ram's son, Ishma**e**l.

2. _____ Sarah gav**e** birth to Abraham's son, Isaac.

3. _____ Abram and Sa**r**ai went to Egypt because there was a fam**i**ne in Canaan.

4. _____ God changed Abram'**s** name to Abraham and established circumcision as the sign of the covenant.

5. _____ Abraham asked the Lord not to kill the **i**nnocent with the guilty in So**d**om.

6. _____ As a test of faith, God told Abraham to take his son, Isaac, and offer him up as a s**a**crifice.

7. _____ A**b**ram went with his father, Terah, to Haran.

8. _____ Abra**h**am bought a piece of land as a burial place for Sarah.

9. _____ After the defeat of the four kings, Melchizedek brought bread and w**i**ne to Abra**m**.

10. _____ Abram and Lot parted ways and s**e**parated their belongings.

11. _____ Abraham and **A**bimelech made a pact at Beer-sheba.

12. _____ The Lord called Abram to leave his father's ho**u**se in Haran and travel to Canaan.

13. _____ Abram save**d** his nephew, Lot, who **h**ad been taken as a prisoner by four kings.

14. _____ After the birth of Isaac, Abraham **s**ent Hagar and Ishmael away.

Abraham lived a full life, and when he died, his sons Isaac and Ishmael

— — — — — —   — — —

— — — — — —   — — — — — .

(Genesis 25:7–10)

Abraham

Abram and his wife, Sarai, were nomads who moved from place to place looking for grass for their sheep and goats. One day God told them to leave the land of Ur—the land of their families—and move to a new land far away. God told Abram that he would give him this land and that he would make Abram and Sarai the parents of many nations, with descendants as numerous as the stars. This seemed impossible because Abram and Sarai were childless and already quite old.

But Abram believed God, so God made a covenant with him to seal the promise. God also changed Abram's name to Abraham, which means "father of a multitude." Abraham traveled to the new land God had promised. He had many adventures in his travels, including fighting to free his nephew Lot and his family and having to move his family and herds to Egypt during a famine.

Abraham had many opportunities to lose faith in God's promise. Twenty-five years passed before he and Sarah (Sarai) gave birth to a son. Then God told Abraham to sacrifice the boy, named Isaac. With complete trust in God, Abraham went to sacrifice Isaac. At the last second, God stopped Abraham and gave him a sheep to sacrifice instead of Isaac.

Abraham is one of the most important characters in the Bible because most of the other stories in the Bible are about his descendants, including Jesus. Because of his strong faith, Abraham is honored as the father of all believers by Jews, Christians, and Muslims—truly a multitude as numerous as the stars.

REFLECTION

Answer these questions after you have read about Abraham.

1. Do you think Abram and Sarai had a hard time leaving their home for a new land? You face similar challenges when going to a new school, neighborhood, or team. How could you make faith a part of your next move?

2. Contracts are business agreements and appear in legal papers, and covenants are sacred promises such as the vows exchanged in marriage ceremonies. Why does God make a covenant rather than a contract with Abraham? Can Abraham keep his side of the covenant without God's help? Can we?

Bible Passages about Abraham

Genesis 12:1–9
God calls Abram to leave Ur.

Genesis 15:1–21
God makes a Covenant with Abram.

Genesis 17:1–16
God changes Abram's and Sarai's names and requests circumcision.

Genesis 18:1–15
God promises to send Sarah and Abraham a son.

Genesis 21:1–8
The birth of Isaac

Genesis 22:1–19
God commands Abraham to sacrifice Isaac.

Breakthrough! Articles

Read these articles to learn more about Abraham.

Breakthrough! Interview with Abraham

An Act of Faith
Genesis 12:1–9

Fear and Faith
Genesis 15:1–15

What's in a Name?
Genesis 17:1–22

Surprises from God
Genesis 18:1–15

The Ultimate Sacrifice
Genesis 22:1–19

Name: _____

Sarah

Using the clues as help, unscramble the jumbled words. For each clue, write the correct word in the spaces, one letter to a space. Some letters are assigned numbers. Using those numbers, fill in the blanks at the bottom to learn how God treated Sarah.

1. Sarah's name, at first (Genesis 11:29)

   R A I A S ___ ___ ___ ___ ___
            11   6

2. Sarai moved here from Ur. (Genesis 11:31)

   R N A H A ___ ___ ___ ___ ___
          19   17

3. Sarai traveled to Egypt because of this. (Genesis 12:10)

   E F M N I A ___ ___ ___ ___ ___ ___
            18   3

4. Quality of Sarai that appealed to the Egyptian king (Genesis 12:14–15)

   Y E T A B U ___ ___ ___ ___ ___ ___
          8   1

5. What Sarah did when she heard she would have a child. (Genesis 18:12)

   H U L A G D E ___ ___ ___ ___ ___ ___ ___
          9   14

6. God promised to keep this with the son of Sarah. (Genesis 17:19)

   N O T E C N V A ___ ___ ___ ___ ___ ___ ___ ___
            5   13

7. Son of Sarah and Abraham (Genesis 21:3)

   S I A C A ___ ___ ___ ___ ___
          12 16

8. Son of Hagar whom Sarah had sent away (Genesis 21:8–11)

   E M H A S L I ___ ___ ___ ___ ___ ___ ___
          15 2   4

9. Sarah was buried in a cave at the edge of this. (Genesis 23:19)

   L I D E F ___ ___ ___ ___ ___
           10   7

___ ___ ___   ___ ___ ___ ___
1 2 3   4 5 6 7

___ ___ ___ ___ ___ ___ ___
8 9 10 11 12 13 14

___ ___ ___ ___ ___.
15 16 17 18 19

(Genesis 17:16)

Sarah

We learn about Sarah in the Book of Genesis. When we first meet her, her name is Sarai and her husband's name is Abram. Because this couple has such a special role in God's plan, they both receive new names: Sarah and Abraham.

God promises Abraham and Sarah that they will have a son, but both of them are quite old. They hold out hope for a long time. When Sarah loses hope, she offers Abraham her servant Hagar to be the mother of God's promised son. After Hagar's son, Ishmael, is born, Sarah is jealous of Hagar because Sarah continues to be childless while Hagar has a child. She sends Hagar and Ishmael away even though it was very dangerous for them to leave the tribe.

But God tells Abraham that Sarah is to be the one through whom the divine promise of a nation will come. After years of waiting, the elderly couple conceives and gives birth to Isaac. Sarah is the mother of the Jewish people because they are descendants of her son, Isaac.

Through Sarah, God demonstrates that all things are possible, even pregnancy for an elderly woman! This is just the first of many wonders that God will work for his Chosen People.

REFLECTION

Answer these questions after you have read about Sarah.

1. How does God reveal himself as a God of surprises in the story of Sarah? When has God surprised you?

2. It was shameful in Sarah's culture not to bear children. Why does the culture's belief make it extra hard for her to believe in God's promises? What are some cultural values today that make it hard to believe in God's words and promises?

3. What are the strengths and weaknesses that you see in Sarah's character? How did her strengths help her relationship with God, and how did her weaknesses get in the way of this relationship? What strengths do you have that can help you in your relationship with God?

Bible Passages about Sarah

Genesis 12:10–20
Sarai, Abram's wife or sister?

Genesis 16:1–6
Sarai tries to control family plan.

Genesis 17:1–22
God corrects family plan.

Genesis 18:1–15
God's promise

Genesis 21:1–8
Birth of Isaac

Breakthrough! Articles

Read these articles to learn more about Sarah.

***Breakthrough!* Interview with Sarah**

An Act of Faith
Genesis 12:1–9

What's in a Name?
Genesis 17:1–22

Surprises from God
Genesis 18:1–15

Jealousy
Genesis 21:9–21

Name: _____

Isaac

Below are three statements, written in code, about Isaac. Each letter of the alphabet is represented by a symbol. The same symbol represents the same letter in all statements. Read Genesis 17:19,21; Genesis 25:19–34; and Genesis 27:1–29 and then try to decode the statements. To get you started, the symbols for eight consonants and all the vowels have been provided.

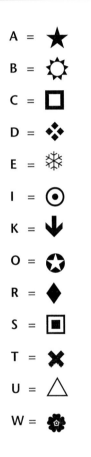

A = ★
B = ☼
C = ◻
D = ❖
E = ❈
I = ◉
K = ↓
O = ✪
R = ◆
S = ◼
T = ✖
U = △
W = ❀

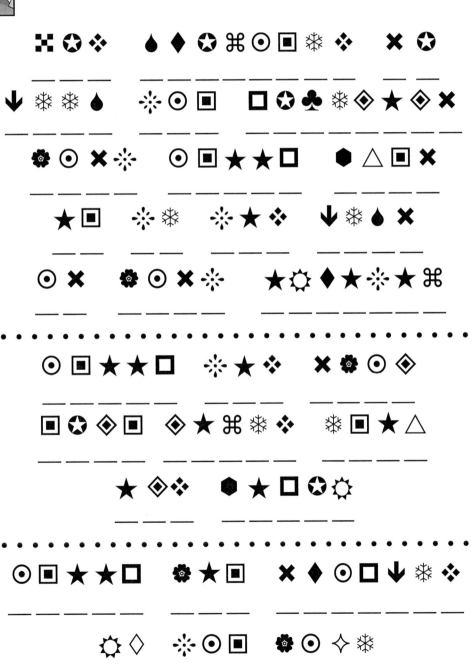

25

Isaac

Isaac is the promised son of Abraham and Sarah. God will continue the covenant he made with Abraham through Isaac. Isaac and his wife, Rebecca, are the parents of Jacob and Esau. Jacob will have twelve sons, who become the fathers of the Twelve Tribes of Israel.

Isaac's remarkable life was guided by God's hand. First, he was born to elderly parents, a sign of God's love and power. When Abraham was called by God to sacrifice Isaac, Isaac was saved at the last minute by a messenger from God. This story taught that God did not require child sacrifice, something required by some of the false gods. Also in this story, Isaac resembles Jesus because he was willing to be humbly sacrificed according to God's will.

God's power is at work when Abraham's servant encounters Rebecca, who becomes Isaac's wife. When Abraham prays to God that Rebecca will have children, she gives birth to twin boys. Even though there is rivalry between the boys, Isaac's blessing from God continues into the next generation through his son Jacob.

Isaac teaches us the importance of trusting in God in all the ordinary and extraordinary events of our lives.

REFLECTION

Answer these questions after you have read about Isaac.

1. As you read through the biblical stories about Isaac, would you say that Isaac's life was (1) full of ups and downs? (2) average in terms of ups and downs? or (3) always the same? Why did you make the choice that you did? How would you rate your own life?

2. Isaac's birth was the result of God's promise to Abraham and Sarah (Genesis, chapter 21). How might your life be different if you lived every day realizing that you too are the result of God's promise?

3. Isaac was tested as well when God asked Abraham to sacrifice him (Genesis, chapter 22). When do you feel tested in small or big ways? Do you look for God in these situations, like Abraham and Isaac did?

Bible Passages about Isaac

Genesis 21:1–8
Isaac's birth

Genesis 22:1–19
Abraham leads Isaac to sacrifice.

Genesis, chapter 24
Isaac's servant brings Rebecca to Isaac.

Genesis 25:19–26
Rebecca gives birth to their sons, Esau and Jacob.

Genesis 25:27–34
Isaac's family dynamics

Genesis 27:1–29
Isaac gives Jacob a blessing rather than Esau.

Breakthrough! Articles

Read these articles to learn more about Isaac.

Breakthrough! Interview with Isaac

What's in a Name?
Genesis 17:1–22

Surprises from God
Genesis 18:1–15

Jealousy
Genesis 21:9–21

The Ultimate Sacrifice
Genesis 22:1–19

A Match Made in Heaven
Genesis 24:57–67

Thanks for Siblings
Genesis 25:19–34

Jacob

Answers to the following clues can be found in the Book of Genesis.
Chapter and verse are given in each clue.

ACROSS

4. Jacob's name was changed to this. (35:10)
6. Jacob's first wife (29:23)
9. Father of Jacob (25:21–26)
10. Esau gave his birthright as firstborn to Jacob for this. (25:29–34)
11. Jacob was holding onto this when he was born. (25:26)
13. Jacob asked Laban to let him go here. (30:25)
14. Jacob met Rachel at this spot. (29:9–14)
18. Jacob's oldest son (35:23)
20. Jacob and his mother plotted to get Isaac to ___ Jacob in place of Esau. (27:6–17)

DOWN

1. Where Jacob told Rachel and Leah to meet him. (31:4)
2. Daughter of Jacob and Leah (30:21)
3. In his dream, Jacob saw a stairway, or ladder, that reached to here. (28:12)
5. Jacob's favorite wife (29:30)
7. This was thrown out of joint on Jacob when he wrestled. (32:25)
8. Rebecca (Rebekah) was the ___ of Jacob. (25:21–26)
12. Jacob and Esau were this. (25:21–26)
15. Jacob's uncle and father-in-law (29:10,21–30)
16. Jacob's first son with Rachel (30:22–24)
17. Number of years Jacob promised to work in order to marry Rachel (29:18)
19. Jacob was afraid to meet him. (32:6–7)

Jacob

Jacob and his twin brother, Esau, were rivals from the time they were in their mother's womb. In fact, when they were born, Jacob came out grabbing Esau's heel. As the firstborn of the twins, Esau was first in line to receive the inheritance and blessing of his father, Isaac. But Jacob persuaded Esau to give Jacob his inheritance rights in exchange for a bowl of stew. Later, Jacob tricked his father into giving him the special blessing that was supposed to be for Esau.

Esau was so angry after this that Jacob fled for his life. Isaac and Rebekah sent him to live with a far-away uncle, Laban. During his journey, God told Jacob in a dream that he and his descendants would receive all the promises of the covenant that God had made with Abraham.

Jacob stayed with his uncle for fourteen years. During that time, he married his uncle's daughters, Leah and Rachel, and made his fortune.

On the journey back to his father's house, Jacob spent an entire night wrestling with a stranger. Only as day began to break did Jacob realize that the stranger was really God! God changed Jacob's name to Israel. His new name became the name of the nation founded by his twelve sons, each of whom was father to one of Israel's Twelve Tribes.

Bible Passages about Jacob

Genesis 25:19–26
The birth of Esau and Jacob to Isaac and Rebecca

Genesis 25:27–34
Esau sells rights as firstborn son.

Genesis 27:1–45
Rebecca and Jacob deceive Isaac and Jacob receives blessing.

Genesis 29:15–30
Jacob marries Leah and Rachel.

Genesis 32:22–30
Jacob receives the name Israel.

Genesis 33:1–20
Jacob meets Esau.

REFLECTION

Answer these questions after you have read about Jacob.

1. "The moral of the story is . . ." What do you think is the moral to the story of Jacob? If you had to make his story into a movie, what would you call it? What would the movie teach people today?

2. Read Genesis 29:1–30 and Genesis 31:1–3,22–30,36–42,55. What kind of relationship does Jacob have with his father-in-law? Which relative of yours do you like the best? How do you and that person make your relationship work well?

3. Jacob says to Esau, "To see your face is for me like seeing the face of God" (Genesis 33:10). Jacob has been afraid that Esau would not forgive him for his actions when he was younger. Describe the way you think Esau's face must have looked to Jacob. When have you seen that look on another person's face?

Breakthrough! Articles

Read these articles to learn more about Jacob.

Breakthrough! **Interview with Jacob**

Thanks for Siblings
Genesis 25:19–34

Esau's Dilemma
Genesis 27:1–29

An Imperfect Believer
Genesis 30:25–43

Jacob's Wrestling Match
Genesis 32:22–32

A Moment of Great Power
Genesis 33:1–11

The Tribe of Judah
Genesis 49:8–12

Leah and Rachel

Read the following "if-then" statements and determine which one is true. Then place the correct letter in the spaces below to find out a fact about Rachel. You can find all the answers in Genesis, chapters 29–31.

If Jacob met Leah at the well, then 7 is R. If Jacob met Rachel at the well, then 7 is L.

If Jacob agreed to work seven years to marry Leah, then 5 is S. If Jacob agreed to work seven years to marry Rachel, then 5 is T.

Leah and Rachel were sisters. If Leah was older than Rachel, then 9 is H. If Rachel was older than Leah, then 9 is M.

If Leah's maid was Zilpah, then 3 is B. If Rachel's maid was Zilpah, then 3 is J.

If Jacob was tricked into marrying Leah, then 6 is H. If Jacob was tricked into marrying Rachel, then 6 is S.

If Jacob loved Leah best, then 1 is A. If Jacob loved Rachel best then, 1 is I.

If Leah's maid was Bilhah then 4 is O. If Rachel's maid was Bilhah, then 4 is E.

If Leah gave birth to Jacob's firstborn son, then 11 is M. If Rachel gave birth to Jacob's firstborn son, then 11 is N.

If Leah was the mother of Joseph, then 10 is U. If Rachel was the mother of Joseph, then 10 is E.

If Leah had trouble getting pregnant at first, then 2 is T. If Rachel had trouble getting pregnant at first, then 2 is N.

If Leah stole her father's household gods, then 8 is A. If Rachel stole her father's household gods, then 8 is E.

Rachel was buried

___ ___ ___ ___ ___ ___ ___ ___ ___ ___ ___.
1   2   3   4   5   6   7   8   9   10   11

Leah and Rachel

Leah and Rachel were the wives of Jacob (also known as Israel). Together with their maids, Zilpah and Bilhah, they bore twelve sons and one daughter for Jacob. The twelve sons were the fathers of the Twelve Tribes of Israel.

Jacob met the sisters when he went to live with his uncle, Laban. Leah and Rachel were Laban's daughters, which made them cousins to Jacob. He met Rachel first and instantly fell in love with her. He promised Laban that he would work for him for seven years in exchange for having Rachel as his wife. At the end of seven years though, Laban tricked Jacob into marrying Leah instead. When Jacob protested Laban's trickery, his uncle gave him Rachel in marriage too—but only in exchange for another seven years of work.

Jacob loved Rachel more than Leah, which caused Leah to resent Rachel. But Leah and her maid, Zilpah, bore twice as many children for Jacob than Rachel and her maid, Bilhah, which made Rachel jealous of Leah. Despite the rivalry between the sisters, they would be forever remembered as the ones God chose to be the mothers of a new nation.

REFLECTION

Answer these questions after you have read about Leah and Rachel.

1. Read the stories about Leah and Rachel. First, consider them as you think Leah experienced them. Then look at them from Rachel's perspective. Do you think their lives were very much alike even though they lived in the same house? Do any two family members share the same experience of their family?

2. Read Genesis 29:9–11. Notice that a stranger (Jacob) to Rachel kisses her upon meeting her for the first time. Kissing may have been the custom then. What kinds of greetings by friends or strangers make you feel comfortable? Are there any that make you feel uncomfortable? Whom might you talk to about this second type?

Bible Passages about Leah and Rachel

Genesis 29:1–14
Rachel meets Jacob for the first time.

Genesis 29:15–20
Jacob works seven years to marry Rachel.

Genesis 29:21–30
Laban tricks Jacob and he marries Leah and Rachel.

Genesis 29:31–35
Leah bears four sons.

Genesis 30:1–21
Leah and Rachel's maidservants bear more children.

Genesis 30:22–24
Rachel gives birth to Joseph.

Genesis 35:16–20
Rachel dies giving birth to Benjamin.

Breakthrough! Article

Read this article to learn more about Leah and Rachel.

Breakthrough! Interview with Leah and Rachel

Name: _____

Joseph

The story of Joseph is significant for many reasons, so it is important to read it carefully. As you read the story, do the math problems below and write your answers in the spaces provided. The problems are in the order in which you find them in the Bible. When you are finished, you will find out something about Joseph.

Joseph had 11 brothers. To that number, add the age of Joseph at the start of his story. (Genesis 37:2) _____

From that number, subtract the number of stars that bowed down to Joseph in his dream. (Genesis 37:5–11) _____

To that number, add the number of silver pieces that his brothers got for selling Joseph. (Genesis 37:28) _____

Multiply that number by the number of prisoners whose dreams Joseph interpreted. (Genesis 40:5–8) _____

Multiply that by the number of days that Joseph tells the baker he has before his head will be chopped off. (Genesis 40:16–19) _____

From that number, subtract the number of lean, or thin, cows in the dream Joseph interpreted. (Genesis 41:17–19) _____

Multiply that by the number of dreams the king (pharaoh) had. (Genesis 41:25) _____

From that number, subtract the age of Joseph when he began service to the king. (Genesis 41:45) _____

Divide that number by the number of sons Joseph had. (Genesis 41:50) _____

Then multiply the number of days Joseph held his brothers in prison (Genesis 42:17) by the amount of food Benjamin was served in comparison to his brothers. (Genesis 43:34) _____; subtract that number from your previous answer in this problem. _____

From that number, subtract the total number of Jacob's family who lived in Egypt. (Genesis 46:27) _____

From that number, subtract the number of Joseph's brothers who went with him to see the king after they settled in Goshen. (Genesis 47:1) _____

If you did the math correctly, your answer should match the number in Genesis 50:26.
Complete the following sentence using that number.

Joseph died at the age of _____.

Joseph

Joseph, one of Jacob's twelve sons, was deeply resented by his brothers. Their father's favoritism toward Joseph was annoying enough, but Joseph made matters worse by boasting of dreams in which his family bowed down before him.

Joseph's brothers finally sold him into slavery in Egypt. There God gave him the ability to correctly interpret the dreams of his fellow prisoners. Word of Joseph's talent eventually reached Pharaoh, who called on Joseph to interpret his own dreams. Joseph predicted that seven years of great prosperity would be followed by seven years of terrible famine. Impressed, Pharaoh placed Joseph in charge of overseeing the entire land for the purpose of storing up enough grain to outlast the famine.

When Joseph's brothers came to Egypt to buy grain during the famine, Joseph hid his identity from them and threatened to make the youngest brother, Benjamin, his slave. When he saw his brothers' brave attempts to save Benjamin from slavery though, Joseph revealed who he was and forgave them. He told them that God had used their evil to save the family from starvation.

By forgiving his brothers rather than getting even with them, Joseph made it possible for the family to prosper in Egypt, and eventually grow into the nation of Israel.

REFLECTION

Answer these questions after you have read about Joseph.

1. When we first meet Joseph in Genesis 37:3–11, we learn that he has at least two special gifts. Which one does his father give him? Which gift does God give him? Ask yourself the same questions: What gifts has God given me? What gifts have other people given me?

2. The story in Genesis 37:12–36 is a pretty serious case of sibling rivalry. Joseph's brothers are so jealous of him that they sell him into slavery! What are the main causes of rivalry between brothers and sisters in families? Are there attitudes or actions that you think can prevent rivalry or make it happen less?

3. Joseph's life has interesting twists and turns. What looks bad at first (like slavery or jail) turns out for the best in the end. Have any of your bad experiences ever turned out to be good experiences later? If so, why?

Bible Passages about Joseph

Genesis 37:1–36
Joseph is sold into slavery.

Genesis 39:1–19
Joseph works for Potiphar and is falsely accused by his wife.

Genesis 39:21—40:23
Joseph is in jail and interprets prisoners' dreams.

Genesis 41:1–36
Joseph interprets Pharaoh's dreams and becomes governor of Egypt.

Genesis, chapters 42–46
Joseph's brothers journey to Egypt and his family moves to Egypt.

Breakthrough! Articles

Read these articles to learn more about Joseph.

Breakthrough! **Interview with Joseph**

Favored Sibling
Genesis, chapter 37

Joseph's Tough Times
Genesis 39:1–6

Catching Dreams
Genesis 41:1–36

The Great River of Blessings
Genesis 42:1–11

The Way to Peace
Genesis, chapter 45

Moses

Put the events of Moses' life in the correct order of how they happened. You can figure this out by scanning the headlines in Exodus, chapters 1–20. Number the events 1 through 14 in the spaces provided. Starting with event number 1, put the bold, underlined letters in the spaces provided at the bottom. Some events have two letters in bold, underlined type. Be sure to put those letters in the spaces in the order in which they appear in the sentence.

1. _____ In a pillar of cloud and a pill__a__r of __f__ire, the Lord guides Moses and the Israelites.

2. _____ J__e__thro and Moses visit.

3. _____ Moses a__nd__ the Israelites arrive at Mount Sinai.

4. _____ Moses and the Is__r__aelites cross the Red Sea.

5. _____ Moses instru__c__ts the peop__le__ on what to do at the first Passover.

6. _____ Moses is __f__loated down a river in a basket.

7. _____ Moses kills __a__ man and flees to Midian.

8. _____ Moses meets __t__he king (pharaoh) of Egypt.

9. _____ Moses receives the Ten Comman__d__ments.

10. _____ Moses warns o__f__ the de__a__th of the firstborn.

11. _____ Water comes from a rock when Moses strikes __it__.

12. _____ The Israelites are led out of Egypt by Mo__se__s.

13. _____ The Lord __c__alls Mos__e__s at the burning bush.

14. _____ The Lord strikes Egypt with plagues, __or__ disasters.

Moses spoke with God

— __ — __ __ __ __ __ __ — __ __ __

__ __ __ __ __ __ __ __ __ __.

Moses

Moses' life is especially interesting because of the many seemingly impossible obstacles he faced. By the time he was born, the Egyptian pharaoh had enslaved the descendants of Jacob and ordered that all the newborn Israelite boys be drowned in the river. Moses was saved from this fate by the pharaoh's daughter, who raised him as her own son.

When Moses was grown, God appeared to him. God wanted Moses to tell the pharaoh to let the Israelites return to the land God had promised Abraham. Moses doubted that he was the right person for the job, but God reminded him that he would have divine help, plus Moses' brother, Aaron, as an assistant.

With God's help Moses led the Israelites in a miraculous escape from the Egyptian army. Once they were free, God worked through Moses to make a covenant with the Israelites, giving them the Ten Commandments to help them keep the covenant.

Leading the Israelites to the Promised Land wasn't easy, especially when the people complained and betrayed God. Moses never entered the Promised Land. But before he died, he reminded the Israelites that if they lived according to the covenant, God would help them overcome even the most impossible obstacles—just as he had done for Moses.

REFLECTION

Answer these questions after you have read about Moses.

1. Often before we receive a punishment such as being grounded or being given a detention, we receive a warning. Sometimes it is pride that keeps us from changing our behavior despite warnings. This may have been true of the Egyptians as well. Through Moses, God gave them warning after warning to let the Israelites go. What warnings does God send to us to change our behavior?

2. Look at the Ten Commandments in Exodus, chapter 20. Choose one Commandment, write it down, and then brainstorm at least five ways we could observe this Commandment in our modern life. Continue this process with the other Commandments.

Bible Passages about Moses

Exodus 2:1–24
Moses' early life

Exodus 3:1–22
God calls Moses.

Exodus 5:1–21
Moses and Aaron before the King of Egypt

Exodus 12:1–4
The Passover

Exodus 14:1–31
Crossing the Red Sea

Exodus 20:1–17
The Ten Commandments

Breakthrough! Articles

Read these articles to learn more about Moses.

Breakthrough! Interview with Moses

Standing Up for Right
Exodus 2:11–17

A God of Many Names
Exodus 3:14

Moses' Problem
Exodus 4:1–17

Now What?
Exodus 5:1–22

Not Me, Lord!
Exodus 6:12–13

On Being Stubborn
Exodus 8:5–19

Promise Breakers and Promise Keepers?
Exodus 9:13–35

Aaron and Miriam

Aaron and Miriam were the brother and sister of Moses.
They assisted Moses during the Exodus.

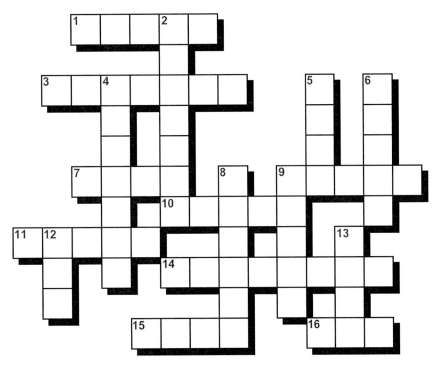

ACROSS

1. Where the Lord spoke to Moses and Aaron (Exodus 12:1)
3. Miriam and Aaron criticized Moses for marrying this kind of woman. (Numbers 12:1)
7. The Lord told Aaron and Miriam to come here. (Numbers 12:4)
9. Aaron could do this well. (Exodus 4:14)
10. Aaron's walking stick turned into this. (Exodus 7:10)
11. Miriam's skin turned this color. (Numbers 12:10)
14. Mother of Miriam (Numbers 26:59)
15. The bull calf that Aaron created was made of this. (Exodus 32:5)
16. Miriam was buried in this wilderness. (Numbers 20:1)

DOWN

2. Aaron and his sons were anointed to be these. (Exodus 30:30)
4. Number of the leaders of Israel who were with Aaron (Exodus 24:1)
5. Aaron and his sons were to set up this in the tent. (Exodus 27:20–21)
6. Father of Aaron (1 Chronicles 23:13)
8. Miriam took her tambourine and did this. (Exodus 15:20)
9. Number of days Miriam was shut out of the camp (Numbers 12:15)
12. Moses, Aaron, and this man went up to the top of the hill. (Exodus 17:10)
13. Tribe, or clan, of Aaron (Numbers 18:1–2)

Aaron and Miriam

Aaron and Miriam are the brother and sister of Moses. They play an important role in the Exodus of the Jewish people from Egypt and their journey in the desert afterward. When Moses was a baby, Moses' mother put him in a basket and put the basket in the river to save his life. Miriam watched over the basket to keep it safe. Later Miriam helped Moses lead the people in their journey from Egypt. The Bible calls her a prophet, and she leads the women in praising God (Exodus 15:20).

Aaron is first a spokesman for Moses while Moses pleads with Pharaoh to let his people go. (Moses would have spoken himself if he were not so insecure about it!) God says that Aaron and his son must be ordained as priests. Their priesthood resembles today's priesthood because they dress in special robes, lead the people in worship of God, and offer sacrifices. But Aaron offers animals for sacrifice while today's Catholic priests offer the sacrifice of Jesus in the Mass. Both Aaron and Moses are descendants of Jacob's son Levi, and are called Levites. Because the priesthood passed from father to son, only Levites would be priests from that time forward.

Despite the honors God bestows on Aaron and Miriam, they are not always faithful in return. When Moses is away and the people demand a visible god to worship, Aaron readily collects gold and creates a golden calf. Aaron and Miriam are also jealous of Moses' close relationship with God and complain about it. But only Miriam is punished with a skin disease (which God heals)!

REFLECTION

Answer these questions after you have read about Aaron and Miriam.

1. What is an idol? What are some idols that people worship today?

2. Were Aaron and Miriam a good brother and sister to Moses? Which stories would cause you to answer yes, and which ones might make you say no? If you have a brother or sister, what kind of job are you doing?

3. Write down the pieces of clothing that Aaron was supposed to wear as a priest in Exodus, chapter 28. Compare these garments with the types of clothes that Roman Catholic priests wear today when saying Mass. Use the dictionary or do some research if necessary.

Bible Passages about Aaron

Exodus 4:14–16,27–30
God speaks to
Moses and Aaron.

Exodus 5:1–4
Moses and Aaron before
the King of Egypt

Exodus 7:1–13
The Lord's command to
Moses and Aaron

Exodus 15:19–21
Miriam's victory song

Exodus 29:1–17
Priestly ordination of
Aaron and his sons

Exodus 32:1–35
The golden calf

Numbers 12:1–16
Aaron and Miriam are
jealous of Moses.

Breakthrough! Articles

Read these articles to learn
more about Aaron and Miriam.

Breakthrough! Interview
with Aaron and Miriam

Moses' Problem
Exodus 4:1–17

***Now* What?**
Exodus 5:1–22

**Promise Breakers and
Promise Keepers?**
Exodus 9:13–35

The Ten Commandments
Exodus 20:1–17

Vestments
Exodus, chapter 28

Sinful but Forgiven
Exodus, chapter 32

Joshua

The story of Joshua starts in the Book of Exodus and continues in the Books of Numbers and Deuteronomy. The biggest part of Joshua's story, however, is found in the Book of Joshua. Answer the following clues about Joshua by looking up the verses indicated after each one. To find out if you are correct, check for each of your answers in the word search. Write the unused letters from the word search in the spaces at the bottom of the page to spell out a fact about Joshua.

1. Joshua went up here with Moses. (8 letters) (Exodus 24:13)

2. Joshua was filled with this. (6 letters) (Deuteronomy 34:9)

3. Joshua sent two spies to go explore this city. (7 letters) (Joshua 2:1)

4. Joshua led the whole nation of Israel across this river. (6 letters) (Joshua 4:1)

5. Joshua ordered the people to shout and march around Jericho this many times. (5 letters) (Joshua 6:15–20)

6. Joshua read this aloud, including the blessings and the curses. (3 letters) (Joshua 8:34)

7. Joshua told the sun to do this. (two words, 10 letters) (Joshua 10:12)

8. Joshua divided the land among all the people of ____. (6 letters) (Joshua 11:23)

9. Joshua defeated many of these. (5 letters) (Joshua 12:7–24)

10. Joshua told the people to revere and honor the ____. (4 letters) (Joshua 24:14)

11. Joshua was buried in this hill country. (7 letters) (Joshua 24:30)

N	M	O	L	O	R	D	S	E	L
S	I	A	P	P	O	I	W	L	O
M	I	A	R	H	P	E	I	N	H
L	T	E	T	D	J	T	S	O	C
S	A	H	U	N	S	A	D	J	I
H	I	W	S	D	U	S	O	O	R
U	S	G	N	I	K	O	M	R	E
L	E	A	R	S	I	C	M	D	J
C	T	E	S	S	O	R	+	A	+
S	N	E	V	E	S	+	+	N	+

__ __ __ __ __   __ __ __ __ __ __ __

__ __ __ __ __ __ __   __ __ __ __

__ __ __ __ __ __ __ __ __ .

Joshua

Soon after the Israelites left Egypt, Moses prepared to lead the people into the Promised Land by sending twelve men ahead to scout the land. They reported that the land was wonderful—flowing "with milk and honey" (Numbers 13:27, NABRE). But most of them advised against going into the land because they thought the inhabitants were too fierce to be defeated. Only two of the scouts, Joshua and Caleb, remembered God's promises and how he had defeated the mighty Egyptian army. They argued that the Israelites could occupy the land if they trusted God.

The Israelites refused to listen to Joshua and Caleb. As a result, they ended up wandering in the desert for many more years before entering the Promised Land.

Before Moses died God commanded him to make Joshua his successor, the new leader of the Israelites. Under Joshua's leadership the Israelites crossed over the Jordan River into the Promised Land. There Joshua led them to victories over the people who lived there. One of his most famous victories was when he led the Israelites in a march around the city of Jericho, which led to the city's walls falling down. As the Bible makes clear, though, all of Joshua's successes came from his unwavering trust in God.

REFLECTION

Answer these questions after you have read about Joshua.

1. After reading the stories about Joshua, choose three qualities that make him a hero. Can you think of three other heroes or heroines (in history, "real life," film, or books) that also possess those qualities? What can all four of these heroes teach you?

2. Read Joshua 24:14–28. The Israelites promise to be faithful to God over and over. Words are very powerful. (Think of gossip!) Why is it important to be faithful to the words of the promises we make to others and to God?

Bible Passages about Joshua

Joshua, chapter 3
Crossing the Jordan River

Joshua, chapter 6
The fall of Jericho

Joshua 11:16–23
The extent of
Joshua's conquest

Joshua 24:1–28
Joshua leads the renewal
of the Covenant.

Joshua 24:29–31
Joshua dies.

Breakthrough! Articles

Read these articles to learn more about Joshua.

***Breakthrough!* Interview with Joshua**

Big Shoes to Fill
Joshua 1:1–9

Remember When . . .
Joshua 3:14–17

Courage
Joshua 8:1–2

Conquering Canaan
Joshua, chapter 12

Older and Wiser
Joshua 13:1–7

Remembering God's Goodness
Joshua 24:1–15

Deborah

Below are three statements, written in code, about Deborah. Each letter of the alphabet is represented by a symbol. The same symbol represents the same letter in all statements. Read Judges, chapters 4–5, then try to decode the statements. To get you started, the symbols for eight consonants and all the vowels have been provided.

A = ★
D = ❖
E = ❄
G = ▨
H = ☀
I = ◉
O = ✪
P = ◆
R = ◆
S = ▣
T = ✖
U = △
W = ✿

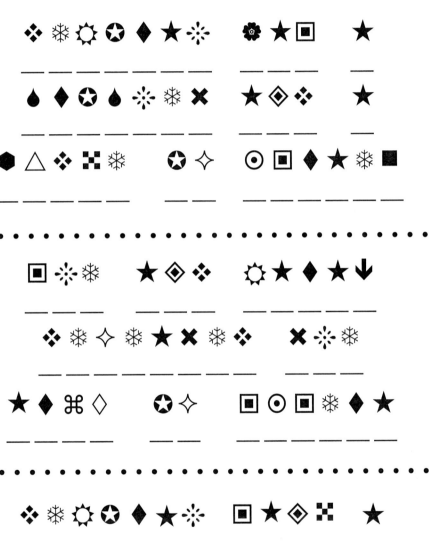

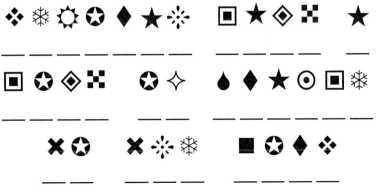

Deborah

Although many of the Israelites' leaders and heroes were men, several women also stand out, including Deborah. She was a prophet and a judge—a spirit-filled leader who accomplished God's justice—during the time after Joshua died, when the Israelites were settling into the Promised Land.

During this time a Canaanite king named Jabin oppressed the Israelites for twenty years. Deborah told Barak, one of the Israelites' military leaders, that God wanted him to go to battle against the king's army. Barak replied that he would go into battle only if Deborah went along. She agreed, but warned him that because he failed to trust God's Word, it would be a woman, not him, who would defeat the enemy commander.

As Deborah had predicted, Barak's army defeated the Canaanite army. The commander of the Canaanite army, Sisera, fled the battlefield and hid in the tent of a woman named Jael. Sisera thought he would be safe there, but Jael killed him while he slept and gave his body to Barak.

In response to this victory, Deborah sings an elaborate prayer-song that celebrates how God works through people who are not expected to be heroes, people like Deborah and Jael.

REFLECTION

Answer these questions after you have read about Deborah.

1. In Judges 4:5 we read that people go to Deborah for help with decision making. She is wise because she listens to God. What are some decisions you are making now, small or big? Is there an adult who prays and listens to God who could help you sort through your decisions?

2. Though some people, like Deborah, are very wise, all of us grow in wisdom as time passes. What are two or three bits of wisdom you have gained in the past year?

Bible Passages about Deborah

Judges 4:4–5
Introduction to Deborah, the prophetess and judge

Judges 4:6–16
Deborah calls on Barak to lead the army.

Judges 4:17–24
Jael kills Sisera.

Judges, chapter 5
Deborah and Barak sing God's praises.

Breakthrough! Articles

Read these articles to learn more about Deborah.

Breakthrough! **Interview with Deborah**

A Brave and Wise Woman
Judges 4:1–8

Sing a Song
Judges, chapter 5

Gideon

Gideon was a judge of Israel. His story is found in Judges, chapters 6–8. Read his story and then complete this activity by filling in the answers to the clues below. Put one letter on each line or in the box. When you have completed the activity, the letters in the box will spell out a name vertically. Use that name to answer the question at the bottom.

1. ☐ __ __ __ __

2. __ __ __ ☐ __

3. __ __ ☐ __

4. __ __ __ __ __ ☐ __ __ __ __ __

5. __ __ ☐ __ __ __ __ __ __

6. __ __ __ ☐

7. __ __ __ __ ☐ __ __ __ __

8. __ __ __ ☐ __

9. __ ☐ __ __ __

What does this name have to do with Gideon? _____

_____

CLUES

1. The father of Gideon
2. Supernatural being who visited Gideon
3. Gideon's men blew horns, or trumpets, and broke these to frighten the enemy.
4. Number of men the Lord allowed Gideon to take to battle
5. Son of Gideon
6. Either prince of Midian killed by Gideon
7. These people were ruling Israel when Gideon was called to be a judge.
8. Village of Gideon
9. Gideon tore down one of these built by his father.

Gideon

Gideon's name meant "the cutter." He was the fifth judge—a spirit-filled leader—of Israel. During Gideon's time a people known as Midianites ruled over the Promised Land. Gideon encountered the angel of the Lord, who told Gideon that God was sending him to free the Israelites from the Midianites' rule. At night, in secret, Gideon destroyed the altars and sacred pole of the false god and goddess. The people of his town wanted to kill Gideon for this, but Gideon's father, Joash, stopped the crowd. Joash pointed out that if Baal were really a god, he'd deal with Gideon himself.

After this Gideon rallied the Israelites to fight the Midianites. At one point Gideon had 32,000 warriors, but God made Gideon send away all but 300 of them. With those 300 warriors, God gave Gideon victory over the Midianite army.

Despite these signs from God, Gideon was not a perfect model of faith. After his victories over the Midianites, he collected gold earrings from the Israelites and made an idol. Following Gideon's lead, the people abandoned God and worshipped the idol. The story shows how hard it was for the first Israelites to completely trust God.

REFLECTION

Answer these questions after you have read about Gideon.

1. When we first read about the Israelites and the Midianites in Judges, chapter 6, would you say that the Israelites are being bullied by the Midianites? Why? What types of behavior do bullies have? From the biblical story, do you think that God is in favor of bullying?

2. As you read over Judges, chapters 6 and 7, notice the conversation that Gideon has with God. If you could talk with God, would you ask for some sort of proof that what he was saying was true? Why or why not? What else would you tell God?

3. Would you call Gideon's conversation with God in Judges, chapter 6 "prayer"? After all, he is talking with God. Does God allow us to express doubts and fears in prayer? In prayer, do we have to "look good" for God?

Bible Passages about Gideon

Judges 6:1–10
The Israelites' relationship to the Midianites

Judges 6:11–40
Gideon asks God for proof.

Judges 7:1–25
Gideon defeats the Midianites.

Judges 8:1–28
The final defeat of the Midianites

Judges 8:29–35
The death of Gideon

Breakthrough! Articles

Read these articles to learn more about Gideon.

Breakthrough! Interview with Gideon

But Lord . . .
Judges 6:11–16

Miracles
Judges 6:17–22,36–40

I Will Not Rule Over You
Judges 8:22–23

Prayer of a Humble Leader
Judges, chapter 9

Samson

Samson was a judge of Israel. His story is in Judges, chapters 13–16. Read the story, and then complete the following activity. Cut out and rearrange the boxes to reveal facts about Samson.

In Judges 13:14, we find that:

NE		NOT	DRIN	WAS	K WI	F SA
ER O	MSON	MOTH	TO	THE		

In Judges 14:6, we find that:

AND S	WIT	S BA	RE H	APAR	SAMS
ORE	T A	LION	ON T	H HI	

In Judges 15:14, we find that:

REAK	TO B	D MA	UGH	AMSO	THE
RONG	HAT	ES T	HIM	ENO	THE
HELD	N ST	LOR	ROP	DE S	

In Judges 16:29–30, we find that:

ILDI	A BU	ED D	SAMS	NOCK	OWN
S	ON K	ILIS	ND K	E PH	TINE
NG A	ILLE	D TH			

Samson

Samson was a sort of biblical superhero, but a flawed one. He had an enormously strong body (he once killed a lion with his bare hands!), but his spirit was often weak. He was a judge, or spirit-filled leader, of Israel.

Samson's mother was unable to have children for a long time. She was so thankful that God answered her prayers for a son that she dedicated Samson to God by raising him as a nazirite. As a sign of their special commitment to God, nazirites did not cut their hair, drink alcohol, or touch dead bodies.

Samson did not always follow those vows, often got in trouble as a result of his weakness for women, and sometimes used his strength for selfish reasons. Even so, God used him to fight the Philistines, the Israelites' enemy at the time. In one story, for instance, he killed one thousand Philistines with the jawbone of a donkey.

Samson fell in love with a Philistine woman, Delilah, who persuaded him to reveal the secret of his strength. He told her that if his long hair were cut, he would lose his strength, because his long hair symbolized his commitment to God. Delilah betrayed Samson by cutting his hair while he slept. The Philistines captured him, tortured him, and made fun of him in their temple. But Samson prayed to God for help, and in one last burst of strength, Samson brought down the temple on his enemies and himself.

REFLECTION

Answer these questions after you have read about Samson.

1. Samson is really a strong man like modern-day wrestlers or boxers. If you had to give Samson a name that his agent could use for publicity, what would it be? The descriptive title should come from his story. (An example would be "Samson, the long-haired hero.") Why did you choose this title?

2. When Samson gets angry, he gets even. What is your experience of anger that seeks to get even? Does anger solve problems? Does getting back at someone ever cause more problems?

Bible Passages about Samson

Judges 13:1–24
An angel announces Samson's birth to his parents.

Judges 14:1–20
Samson marries a Philistine woman who betrays him.

Judges 15:1–8
Samson burns down the Philistines' orchards and fields.

Judges15:9–20
Samson defeats the Philistines with a donkey's jawbone.

Judges 16:4–22
Delilah betrays Samson.

Judges 16:23–31
The death of Samson and the defeat of the Philistines

Breakthrough! Articles

Read these articles to learn more about Samson.

Breakthrough! **Interview with Samson**

A Sneak Preview
Judges 13:2–24

Samson in Trouble
Judges 14:15—15:8

Be Careful Whom You Trust
Judges 16:4–22

Prayer in Despair
Judges 16:23–31

Name: _____

Ruth

The Book of Ruth is a short but moving story of a young woman and her loyalty to her family. After reading Ruth, read the following "if-then" statements. Determine which statement is true and then write the correct letters, in order, in the spaces below to find out a fact about Ruth.

If Elimelech and Naomi moved because of a famine, then 7 is R. If they moved because of an earthquake, then 7 is H.

If Ruth was a Moabite, then 3 is E. If Ruth was an Israelite, then 3 is I.

If Ruth's mother-in-law was Orpah, then 1 is T. If her mother-in-law was Naomi, then 1 is G.

If Ruth returned to her own people, then 5 is K. If Ruth went with Naomi to Judah, then 5 is T.

If Ruth continued to worship her own gods, then 13 is A. If Ruth chose the God of her mother-in-law, then 13 is T.

If Ruth went to Jerusalem, then 10 is S. If Ruth went to Bethlehem, then 10 is D.

If Boaz was the king, then 6 is V. If Boaz was a relative of Naomi, then 6 is G.

If Ruth was forced to work in the fields, then 8 is I. If Ruth volunteered to work in the fields, then 8 is A.

If Ruth helped plant the crop, then 2 is H. If Ruth walked behind the workers, picking up grain, then 2 is R.

If Boaz told Ruth to work in his fields because she was a foreigner, then 4 is N. If Boaz told her to work in his fields because of all she had done for Naomi, then 4 is A.

If Naomi advised Ruth not to work in Boaz's fields, then 9 is D. If Naomi told Ruth to continue working in Boaz's fields, then 9 is N.

If Naomi planned to trick Boaz into giving them more food, then 11 is L. If Naomi planned to get Ruth married, then 11 is M.

If Naomi told Ruth to lie at Boaz's feet, then 16 is R. If Ruth told Naomi to lie at Boaz's feet, then 16 is S.

If Noami's closest relative gave Boaz his sandal, then 15 is E. If Ruth gave Boaz her sandal, then 15 is U.

If Ruth married Boaz, then 12 is O. If Ruth married a closer relative, then 12 is Y.

If Ruth had a son named Obed, then 14 is H. If Ruth had a daughter named Jesse, then 14 is F.

Ruth was the

___ ___ ___ ___ ___ - ___ ___ ___ ___ ___ ___ ___ ___ ___ ___ ___
1   2   3   4   5   6   7   8   9 10 11 12 13 14 15 16

of King David.

Ruth

Ruth was the great-grandmother of King David and a direct ancestor of Jesus. Despite her key role in Israel's history, Ruth was not from Israel. She was from Moab, a neighbor and sometimes enemy of Israel.

During a famine an Israelite family moved to Moab. The family's two sons married Moabite women, Orpah and Ruth. Soon the father died, leaving his wife, Naomi, to rely on her sons for support. But within ten years, the sons had died as well.

In ancient Israel any legal rights or means of support a woman had came from her relationship with a man—a husband, father, brother, or son. Naomi decided to return to Israel, and told her daughters-in-law to return to their parents. But Ruth would not abandon Naomi. Instead she pledged to stay with Naomi forever. That was quite a promise, because as an unmarried foreigner, Ruth would have little status in Israel.

Back in Israel, Naomi and Ruth encountered Boaz, a wealthy relative of Naomi's dead husband. With some encouragement from Naomi, Ruth made herself known to Boaz, who agreed to marry her.

Ruth's story is an example of what true friendship looks like—and a challenge to everyone who might think that "outsiders" are beyond God's care.

REFLECTION

Answer these questions after you have read about Ruth.

1. Ruth is an ordinary person who helps her mother-in-law, Naomi, in an extraordinary way. When have you seen ordinary people do extraordinary things? Could you?

2. Naomi's people warmly welcomed Ruth and spoke well of her. How welcoming is the United States when people immigrate? Do people from different places receive a warm welcome? How can you be welcoming to new people?

Bible Passages about Ruth

Ruth 1:1–5
Introducing the people and the places

Ruth 1:6–22
Naomi's sad situation and Ruth's generous response

Ruth 2:1–23
Ruth gathers grain in Boaz's field.

Ruth 3:1–16
Ruth seeks to marry Boaz.

Ruth 4:1–12
Ruth marries Boaz.

Breakthrough! Articles

Read these articles to learn more about Ruth.

***Breakthrough!* Interview with Ruth**

When Bad Things Happen
Ruth, chapter 1

Caring for Poor People
Ruth 2:1–3

A Good Reputation
Ruth 2:11–12

Marriage Then and Now
Ruth 4:1–12

Samuel

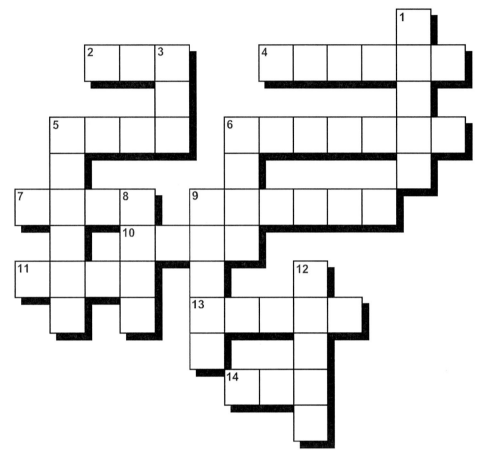

ACROSS

2. Number of books that are named after Samuel

4. Samuel ruled, or judged, ___ throughout his lifetime. (1 Samuel 7:15)

5. The Lord told Samuel to make this man king. (1 Samuel 9:15–17)

6. All Israel knew that Samuel was this. (1 Samuel 3:20)

7. Samuel did not want Israel to have this. (1 Samuel 8:6)

9. Mother of Samuel (1 Samuel 1:19–20)

10. Samuel said it is better to do this than give offerings and sacrifice. (1 Samuel 15:22)

11. The ___ called Samuel. (1 Samuel 3:4)

13. Hometown of Samuel (1 Samuel 25:1)

14. The boy Samuel served the Lord under this priest. (1 Samuel 3:1)

DOWN

1. This many days passed before Samuel came to make the offering at Gilgal. (1 Samuel 13:8)

3. Samuel anointed Saul with this. (1 Samuel 10:1)

5. Where the Lord appeared to Samuel (1 Samuel 3:21)

6. Samuel said he would do this on behalf of Israel. (1 Samuel 7:5)

8. Samuel told Israel to get rid of these things. (1 Samuel 7:3)

9. The Lord does not see what people see; the Lord sees this instead. (1 Samuel 16:7)

12. Samuel anointed him in the presence of his brothers. (1 Samuel 16:13)

Samuel

Samuel was born to a childless woman, Hannah, who dedicated him to God. When Samuel was just three years old, Hannah brought him to live at the shrine at Shiloh. There the young Samuel was instructed by Eli, the priest.

In addition to being a priest and a judge (or leader) for the Israelites, Samuel was also a prophet. He first heard God's voice while he was still a young man serving Eli, and he would continue to speak with God on behalf of the people throughout his life.

When Samuel grew old, the people asked him to appoint a king over them. Samuel did not like this suggestion; after all, the Israelites were supposed to be ruled by God, who was their king. He warned the people about the difficulties they would experience under a king, but the people insisted, and finally God told Samuel to anoint a man named Saul as king.

Samuel told Saul what God wanted him to do. But when Saul disobeyed God, God told Samuel to anoint another king. So Samuel secretly anointed a boy named David as king.

Although he reluctantly anointed Israel's first kings, Samuel made clear that no one—not even a king—rules alone; ultimately, even the most powerful leader must submit to God's rule.

REFLECTION

Answer these questions after you have read about Samuel.

1. Hannah's great desire is to have a son. In her prayer, however, she offers him back to God. What is your most treasured gift from God? Could you put that gift completely into God's hands? What would it take for you to do that?

2. Like the judge Samson, Samuel is a nazirite, someone dedicated to God in a special way. This dedication is obvious to other people because of Samuel's uncut hair and refusal to drink alcohol. Could other people tell anything about your relationship with God from your appearance? Do you wear certain things that might give others the wrong impression about that relationship?

Bible Passages about Samuel

1 Samuel 1:1–18
Hannah prays for a son.

1 Samuel 1:19–28
Samuel is born, and Hannah brings him to the house of the Lord.

1 Samuel 3:1–18
The Lord appears to Samuel.

1 Samuel 7:2–17
Samuel leads the Israelites.

1 Samuel 8:4–21
The people ask Samuel for a king.

1 Samuel 12:1–25
Samuel's final address to the people

Breakthrough! Articles

Read these articles to learn more about Samuel.

***Breakthrough!* Interview with Samuel**

Introduction to First Samuel

Speak, Lord
1 Samuel 3:1–10

Who's the King?
1 Samuel, chapter 8

Being Anointed
1 Samuel 10:1

The Heart of the Matter
1 Samuel 16:1–13

Name: _____

Saul

Saul was the first king of Israel. His story is in 1 Samuel.

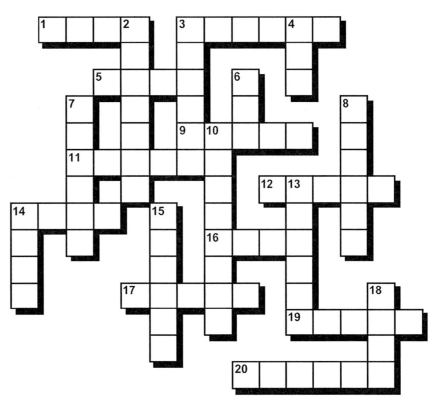

ACROSS

1. David would play this for Saul when Saul was feeling bad. (1 Samuel 16:23)
3. Mount where Saul died (1 Samuel 31:1–6)
5. Saul wanted to ___ David. (1 Samuel 18:17; 19:1)
9. Commander of Saul's army (1 Samuel 17:55)
11. Saul led his people in this. (1 Samuel 11:11)
12. Number of days Saul waited for Samuel to offer sacrifice (1 Samuel 13:8)
14. Father of Saul (1 Samuel 9:1–2)
16. Saul spared this king's life. (1 Samuel 15:9)
17. He was the armor carrier for Saul. (1 Samuel 16:21)
19. In a jealous rage, Saul threw this at David. (1 Samuel 18:11)
20. Saul's story is found in the First Book of _____.

DOWN

2. Saul ordered them killed because he was jealous of David. (1 Samuel 22:13–18)
3. Place where Saul was proclaimed king (1 Samuel 11:15)
4. Samuel used this to anoint Saul. (1 Samuel 10:1)
6. Jonathan, to Saul (1 Samuel 13:2)
7. Saul was buried here. (1 Samuel 31:12–13)
8. Saul's home (1 Samuel 10:26)
10. Tribe of Saul (1 Samuel 9:21)
13. When Saul died, David praised Jonathan and Saul as being "swifter than ____, stronger than lions." (2 Samuel 1:23)
14. Saul's position in Israel (1 Samuel 11:14)
15. Saul disobeyed God because he was ___ of the people. (1 Samuel 15:24)
18. Physical characteristic of Saul (1 Samuel 9:2, 10:23)

Saul

Saul was anointed as Israel's first king by the prophet Samuel. The Israelites wanted to unite all the tribes under a single king because their enemies, the Philistines, were persecuting them.

The Bible contains two different stories about how Saul was anointed king. In one story he sets out to find his father's lost donkeys but instead finds the prophet Samuel, who secretly anoints him. In a less favorable account, the people demand a king, even though Samuel says that a king will cause them trouble and that they should let God be their ruler. According to that story, Saul has to be dragged out of hiding before he can be anointed king.

Things started out well for Saul; he won a great victory against the Ammonites, for instance. But a young man named David soon proved better at fighting the Philistines than Saul, and Saul started ignoring Samuel, God's prophet. Because Saul turned away from God, God told Samuel to anoint another king: David. Saul grew so jealous of David that he tried to kill him, and nearly went mad trying. In the end Saul committed suicide after being badly wounded in a battle with the Philistines, and David was made king.

REFLECTION

Answer these questions after you have read about Saul.

1. Saul goes downhill from when we first meet him until his death. Do you think that he had to go down this path, or could he have made some different choices? Are there any signs when a person is taking a direction in life that will harm her or him?

2. When Saul's spirit is troubled, David plays the harp for him. What songs or types of music help calm you or give you hope? List a few. Why does music have this power for us?

3. Saul tragically commits suicide to avoid being killed by his enemies. People who are depressed or are otherwise really struggling can be at risk for suicide too. Find out what the number is for your local suicide hotline, and identify three adults you could consult if you or a friend were in danger of suicide. Remember, never handle suicide situations by yourself. Always involve an adult.

Bible Passages about Saul

1 Samuel 9:1–18; 10:1,17–24
Samuel encounters Saul and anoints him as king.

1 Samuel 15:1–26
Saul is rejected as king.

1 Samuel 16:14–23
David in Saul's court as harpist

1 Samuel 18:6–16
Saul is jealous of David.

1 Samuel 26:1–25
David spares Saul's life.

1 Samuel 31:1–11
Saul commits suicide.

Breakthrough! Articles

Read these articles to learn more about Saul.

***Breakthrough!* Interview with Saul**

Tall Saul
1 Samuel 9:2

Who Do You Think You Are?
1 Samuel 15:17–25

The Power of Music
1 Samuel 16:14–23

The Jealousy Monster
1 Samuel, chapter 19

A Tragic End
1 Samuel, chapter 31

Name: _____

David

The story of King David is told in detail in the Bible. This activity uses analogies to teach about David's life. An analogy is a comparison showing how the relationship between two people or things is like the relationship between two other people or things. Here is an example of an analogy.

Abraham is to Isaac • as Jacob is to Joseph.

How do Abraham and Isaac compare with Jacob and Joseph? Abraham is the father of Isaac, and Jacob is the father of Joseph.

Complete the following analogies regarding people, places, and events in David's life. The Scripture references in parentheses will help you discover the relationship.

1. Jonathan is to Saul

   as Amnon is to _____.

   (1 Samuel 13:16)

   (2 Samuel 3:2)

2. Kish is to Saul

   as _____ is to David.

   (1 Samuel 9:1–2)

   (1 Samuel 17:12)

3. Samuel is to Saul

   as _____ is to David.

   (1 Samuel 10:1–2)

   (1 Samuel 16:13)

4. Jonathan is to Michal

   as Absalom is to _____.

   (1 Samuel 14:49)

   (2 Samuel 13:1)

5. Nabal is to Abigail

   as Uriah is to _____.

   (1 Samuel 25:14,39–42)

   (2 Samuel 11:2–3,26–27)

6. Saul is to the Ammonites

   as David is to the _____.

   (1 Samuel 11:11)

   (2 Samuel 8:1)

7. Jerusalem is to Solomon

   as _____ is to David.

   (2 Samuel 5:14)

   (1 Samuel 17:12–15)

8. Nathan is to a prophet

   as Joab is to a _____.

   (2 Samuel 7:2)

   (2 Samuel 8:16)

David

It is not surprising that the Israelites remembered David as their greatest leader, given everything he did. He defeated the enemies of Israel on all sides and expanded its territory, bringing peace and prosperity to the land. He united the Twelve Tribes into one nation, and conquered the city of Jerusalem and made it the capital. He brought the Ark of the Covenant to Jerusalem, making it a holy city for all of Israel.

David is also remembered for his great devotion to God. He was a skilled musician who loved to praise God in song and dance; he wrote some of the earliest psalms. As a young man, his total trust in God made it possible for him to defeat the Philistine giant, Goliath. Out of respect for God, he refused to harm King Saul when Saul was trying to kill him. Even when he committed adultery and murder, David admitted his sins, accepted the consequences, and recommitted himself to God.

David was such a great king that, after he died, the Israelites longed for another leader just like him. They called this hoped-for leader the Messiah. Christians believe that this wish came true (although not quite the way many people expected) in Jesus, who was a descendant of David.

REFLECTION

Answer these questions after you have read about David.

1. Who did everyone expect to win the battle between David and Goliath? Why did David win? What are some of the "Goliaths" you face in your own life? What can you learn from this story to apply to the battles in your own life?

2. Read about the friendship between David and Jonathan in 1 Samuel 18:1–5; 1 Samuel 20:1–42; and 2 Samuel 9:1–13. How was Jonathan loyal to David? In 1 Samuel 20:42, we learn that God was part of their friendship. How is God a part of your friendships? How could God be an even greater part of those relationships?

3. Many of the psalms were written by David. Browse through the Book of Psalms and stop when you find one you would like to read. Read the psalm like a prayer. If David were going to pray with us through music today, how might that same psalm look and sound?

Bible Passages about David

1 Samuel 16:1–13
Samuel anoints David as king.

1 Samuel 17:41–54
David defeats Goliath.

1 Samuel 24:1–22
David spares Saul's life.

2 Samuel 5:1–16
David becomes king of Israel and Judah.

2 Samuel 7:1–17
Nathan sends a message to David about a temple.

2 Samuel 11:1–27
David seduces Bathsheba.

2 Samuel 12:1–15
Nathan's message and David's repentance

Breakthrough! Articles

Read these articles to learn more about David.

Share and Share Alike
1 Samuel 30:17–25

Torn Apart
2 Samuel 1:1–12

It's a Party!
2 Samuel 6:12–23

An Eternal Kingdom
2 Samuel 7:12–29

Facing the Truth
2 Samuel, chapters 11–12

Fathers and Sons
2 Samuel 13:1–21

The Man Whom God Made Great
2 Samuel 23:1

Name: _____

Solomon

The story of King Solomon is in 1 Kings, chapters 1–11. To complete the statements below, read the passages indicated at the end of each sentence. To find out if you are correct, check for each of your answers in the word search. Put the unused letters from the word search in the spaces at the bottom of the page to spell out a fact about Solomon. (All passages are in 1 Kings.)

1. Solomon was the son of
   ___ ___ ___ ___ ___. (2:12)

2. God told Solomon he would make him
   ___ ___ ___ ___. (3:12)

3. Solomon built the
   ___ ___ ___ ___ ___ ___. (6:1)

4. The Lord promised Solomon that if Solomon obeyed all God's commands, he would not forsake, or abandon,
   ___ ___ ___ ___ ___ ___. (6:11–13)

5. It took ___ ___ ___ ___ ___ years to build the Temple. (6:38)

6. Solomon also built a
   ___ ___ ___ ___ ___ ___ for himself.
   (7:1)

7. Solomon used
   ___ ___ ___ ___ ___ ___ labor to build the Temple and palace. (9:15)

8. Solomon was visited by the queen of ___ ___ ___ ___ ___. (10:1)

9. The ___ ___ ___ ___ ___ of Solomon led him into worship of other gods. (11:1–4)

10. ___ ___ ___ ___ ___ ___ ___ ___ led a revolt against Solomon. (11:26–27)

11. Solomon was king for ___ ___ ___ ___ ___ years. (11:42)

12. Solomon's son, ___ ___ ___ ___ ___ ___ ___ ___, became king after Solomon. (11:43)

T	S	S	O	L	D	O	J	M	M	O	E
E	N	W	H	W	A	E	A	S	R	I	C
M	C	H	I	E	R	O	C	E	R	A	A
P	N	S	D	O	B	W	I	R	F	S	L
L	E	E	B	O	R	A	T	O	O	D	A
E	H	O	H	L	E	A	R	S	I	F	P
A	A	E	N	A	N	T	Y	V	O	T	H
M	R	E	R	K	Y	I	A	N	G	+	+
N	E	V	E	S	+	D	S	E	V	I	W

___ ___ ___ ___ ___   ___ ___ ___   ___ ___ ___

___ ___ ___   ___ ___ ___ ___ ___ ___ ___

___ ___ ___   ___ ___ ___ ___ ___ ___ ___ ___ .

Solomon

Solomon, the third king of Israel, was famous for his wisdom. Shortly after he became king, God appeared to him in a dream and told him to ask for anything he wanted. Instead of asking for riches or a long life, Solomon asked for the wisdom to be a good ruler. Pleased, God promised him great wisdom—and riches and a long life too.

People came from all over, even from foreign lands, to hear Solomon. The Bible also honors his legendary wisdom by naming him as the author of the Book of Proverbs, the Song of Songs, and Ecclesiastes.

Solomon used his wisdom to strengthen the nation of Israel. He made alliances with other nations by marrying the daughters of foreign kings, and made sure that Israel profited from the trade that passed through its borders. He made Jerusalem a great city with a palace and military defenses. Most important, he built a magnificent Temple for God in Jerusalem.

But all these things came at a great price to the Israelites, who were heavily taxed and forced to work for months on Solomon's building projects. Solomon also turned his heart from God, building altars to the foreign gods and goddesses of his wives. As a result of these things, the northern tribes refused to accept Solomon's son as their king when Solomon died. So the nation of Israel was split into two parts.

REFLECTION

Answer these questions after you have read about Solomon.

1. Read 1 Kings 3:1–10. When God asks Solomon what he wants, he asks for wisdom. What is wisdom? Is wisdom just the same as being smart? If God invited you to ask for whatever you wanted, what would you ask for? Why?

2. God gave Solomon wisdom, power, wealth, and a long life. If you had these four things, what are three things you would do to make the world a better place?

3. In 1 Kings, chapter 6, Solomon begins to build the Temple for God to dwell in. Saint Paul says, "Don't you know that your body is the temple of the Holy Spirit . . . ?" (1 Corinthians 6:19). If the Holy Spirit dwells within us, how should we be caring for our body, mind, and soul? Do you have plans to build your faith so that it is strong?

Bible Passages about Solomon

1 Kings 3:1–15
Solomon prays for wisdom.

1 Kings 3:16–28
Solomon decides wisely for two mothers.

1 Kings 6:1–38
Solomon builds the Temple.

1 Kings 8:54–61
Solomon prays.

1 Kings 10:1–13
The Queen of Sheba visits.

1 Kings 11:1–13
Solomon turns away from God.

Breakthrough! Articles

Read these articles to learn more about Solomon.

Introduction to the First Book of Kings

***Breakthrough!* Interview with King Solomon**

Not a Perfect Person
1 Kings 3:6–9

Three Thousand Proverbs!
1 Kings 4:20–34

A Place to Worship
1 Kings, chapters 5–6

A Royal Visit
1 Kings 10:1–13

Too Many Gods . . . or Wives?
1 Kings 11:1–8

Name: _____

Elijah

Elijah spoke the Word of God to his people and, particularly, to the evil King Ahab and Queen Jezebel. His story is in 1 and 2 Kings. Use the clues to unscramble the words below each clue. When you are finished, write down the letters in the boxes and unscramble those to fill in the two blanks at the bottom of the page.

These birds fed Elijah. (1 Kings 17:2–7)

V S A R E N □ _ _ _ □ _

God chose her to help Elijah. (1 Kings 17:9)

D I W W O □ □ _ _ _

God told Elijah to present himself to this man, who was the king. (1 Kings 18:1–2)

B A H A _ □ _ _

Elijah called for the prophets of Baal to come to this mount. (1 Kings 18:19)

M E R C A L □ _ _ _ _ □

Elijah said he was the only _____ of the Lord left. (1 Kings 18:22)

T H E R P O P □ _ _ □ _ _ _

Elijah took _____ stones to build an altar to the Lord. (1 Kings 18:31–32)

V E L W E T □ □ _ _ _ _

In the quiet, Elijah heard the _____ of the Lord. (1 Kings 19:10–15)

C I V O E _ □ □ _ _

The Lord told Elijah to accuse Ahab of having Naboth murdered in order to take this. (1 Kings 21:1–19)

D V R I A N Y E _ □ _ _ _ □ _ □

A fiery __ __ __ __ __ __ __ came between Elijah and Elisha,

and Elijah went to Heaven in a __ __ __ __ __ __ __ __ __.

Read 2 Kings 2:9–11 to see if your answer is correct.

Elijah

Elijah was a prophet and a miracle worker who lived when the wicked King Ahab and his wife, Jezebel, ruled Israel. Jezebel, the daughter of the king of Tyre, encouraged the Israelites to worship Tyre's god, Baal, and murdered every Israelite prophet she could find—but not Elijah.

Elijah told Ahab that God was sending a great drought as a sign of what would happen if people cut themselves off from God. Elijah hid from Ahab during the drought, staying with a foreign widow for a time. The widow generously provided him with the very last of her food, which God then miraculously replenished for a year.

After three years Elijah challenged the priests of Baal to a contest. He told them to call on Baal to prove that he was real by sending fire down on the priests' sacrifice. All day long the priests called on Baal; Elijah told them to call louder, in case the god was asleep, but nothing happened. Then Elijah poured water over his own sacrifice until it was drenched. When he prayed to God, the sacrifice—and even the altar—was totally consumed by fire.

Elijah's faith in God was so deep that instead of just dying at the end of his life, Elijah was carried directly to Heaven in a flaming chariot.

REFLECTION

Answer these questions after you have read about Elijah.

1. Elijah dares the prophets of Baal to a contest in 1 Kings, chapter 18, so that the people can decide whom to worship. Sometimes it feels like our culture, with its emphasis on beauty, money, and owning things, is daring us to give up our faith in God's importance. Whom do you see and hear in our society challenging people to believe in the one, true God?

2. Read 1 Kings 19:1–8, the story of Elijah's encounter with God in the cave. Notice that Elijah is able to figure out when God is present and when he is not present. When and how do you know that God is present? When and how do you know that God is not present?

Bible Passages about Elijah

1 Kings 17:1–7
Call of Elijah

1 Kings 17:8–24
Elijah goes to see the widow of Zarephath.

1 Kings 18:1–40
Elijah, King Ahab, and the prophets of Baal

1 Kings 19:1–8
Elijah encounters God in a cave on Mount Sinai.

1 Kings 19:19–21
Elijah calls Elisha.

2 Kings 2:1–12
Elijah departs in a flaming chariot.

Breakthrough! Articles

Read these articles to learn more about Elijah.

***Breakthrough!* Interview with Elijah and Elisha**

Elijah
1 Kings, chapters 17–18

A Whisper
1 Kings, chapter 19

Elisha
1 Kings 19:19–21

No Shame
1 Kings, chapter 21

Saying Good-bye
2 Kings 2:1–15

Elisha

Elisha was a prophet and a devoted follower of Elijah. They met while Elisha was working in the fields (1 Kings 19:19–21). After Elijah was taken up to Heaven, Elisha continued Elijah's work. Elisha is known for performing several miracles.

In this activity you will match descriptions of Elisha's miracles to key people or things having to do with those miracles. Read 2 Kings 2:9–25 and 2 Kings 4:1—6:7. Then match the phrases in the list below to the phrases in the boxes, writing the number of the matching phrase in the box. When you finish, the numbers you have put in the boxes should add up to the same total across, up and down, and diagonally.

ELISHA'S MIRACLES

Elisha causes an ax head to float.	Elisha purifies bad water.	Elisha causes one jar, or jug, of oil to fill many jars, or vessels.
Elisha revives someone who has died.	Elisha cures a man of leprosy.	Elisha makes poisoned stew good to eat.
Elisha blesses a childless woman so that she may have a son.	Elisha multiplies loaves and grain.	Elisha divides the Jordan River.

KEY PEOPLE OR THINGS ASSOCIATED WITH ELISHA'S MIRACLES

1. Elisha helps the people of a town.
2. Elisha repays a woman's kind act of providing a room for him.
3. Elisha helps a group of prophets during a famine.
4. Elisha uses Elijah's coat or mantle.
5. Elisha helps an army commander.
6. Elisha helps a man find something he lost.
7. Elisha helps a young boy.
8. Elisha helps a widow whose sons will be sold into slavery.
9. Elisha feeds one hundred men.

Elisha

Elisha was a farmer's son until the day God called him to accompany the prophet Elijah. After Elijah was taken to Heaven, Elisha also became a great prophet.

Like Elijah, Elisha tried to convince the kings of Israel to give up their worship of false gods. One of the ways he did this was by helping the kings fight their enemies. For example, God revealed the battle plans of the Arameans to Elisha, who then told the king of Israel. Frustrated by his defeats, the Aramean king sent soldiers to capture Elisha. But Elisha asked God to blind them, and then led them to the king of Israel before restoring their sight. Elisha told the king not to kill the enemy soldiers, but to make a great feast for them. After that, the Arameans stopped attacking Israel.

Elisha worked many other miracles as well: he brought a widow's dead son back to life, cured a Syrian general of his leprosy, fed one hundred men with twenty loaves of bread, and even retrieved a friend's lost ax head from the river by making it float. For Elisha, the purpose of these miracles was clear: to remind the people of God's power so that they would return to worshipping him alone.

REFLECTION

Answer these questions after you have read about Elisha.

1. In 2 Kings, chapter 2, Elisha's good friend and mentor, Elijah, is taken up to Heaven. Elijah leaves his cloak for Elisha to take. The cloak symbolizes that Elisha has the same authority and power as Elijah. What kind of keepsakes do you have of friends or family who have moved away, or of loved ones who have died? Why are these items symbols for you?

2. In 2 Kings, chapter 5, King Naaman of Syria wants a quicker fix for his skin problems than the process of washing himself seven times in the Jordan River. It is easy to slack off cleaning newly pierced ears, doing physical therapy exercises after a sports injury, or just keeping our teeth clean! Why does God want us to take good care of our bodies?

Bible Passages about Elisha

1 Kings 19:19–21
Elijah calls Elisha.

2 Kings 2:1–14
Elisha receives Elijah's cloak.

2 Kings 4:1–7
Elisha helps a poor widow.

2 Kings 4:9–37
Elisha and the rich woman

2 Kings 5:1–27
Elisha and Naaman

2 Kings 13:14–21
Elisha dies.

Breakthrough! Articles

Read these articles to learn more about Elisha.

***Breakthrough!* Interview with Elijah and Elisha**

Elisha
1 Kings 19:19–21

Saying Good-bye
2 Kings 2:1–15

Elisha the Rescuer
2 Kings 4:1–7

Seek Healing
2 Kings 5:1–14

Mercy, Not Revenge
2 Kings 6:8–23

Refugees
2 Kings 8:1–6

Name: _____

Hezekiah

The story of Hezekiah is in 2 Kings, chapters 18–20. Read the story and fill in the answers on the right using the clues on the left. Some of the answer spaces have numbers under them. If the space has a number, write the letter from that space in the space with the corresponding number at the bottom to complete a sentence about Hezekiah.

Hezekiah was the son of this man.
$\overline{\hspace{0.4cm}}\overline{\hspace{0.4cm}}\overline{\hspace{0.4cm}}$
37   3

Hezekiah became this at age twenty-five.
$\overline{\hspace{0.4cm}}\overline{\hspace{0.4cm}}\overline{\hspace{0.4cm}}$
5   20   29

Hezekiah destroyed the bronze piece, created by Moses, called _____.
$\overline{\hspace{0.4cm}}\overline{\hspace{0.4cm}}\overline{\hspace{0.4cm}}\overline{\hspace{0.4cm}}\overline{\hspace{0.4cm}}\overline{\hspace{0.4cm}}$
14   4

Hezekiah attacked and defeated these people who had territory in Gaza.
$\overline{\hspace{0.4cm}}\overline{\hspace{0.4cm}}\overline{\hspace{0.4cm}}\overline{\hspace{0.4cm}}\overline{\hspace{0.4cm}}\overline{\hspace{0.4cm}}\overline{\hspace{0.4cm}}\overline{\hspace{0.4cm}}$
9   15

Hezekiah ruled over this area.
$\overline{\hspace{0.4cm}}\overline{\hspace{0.4cm}}\overline{\hspace{0.4cm}}$
10   31   23

The messengers from Assyria told the people not to _____ on the Lord.
$\overline{\hspace{0.4cm}}\overline{\hspace{0.4cm}}\overline{\hspace{0.4cm}}$
16   38   39

This prophet visited Hezekiah when he was sick.
$\overline{\hspace{0.4cm}}\overline{\hspace{0.4cm}}\overline{\hspace{0.4cm}}\overline{\hspace{0.4cm}}$
6   18   13   1

Isaiah told Hezekiah to put his house and everything in _____, for he was about to die.
$\overline{\hspace{0.4cm}}\overline{\hspace{0.4cm}}\overline{\hspace{0.4cm}}$
26   28   2

Isaiah told Hezekiah that his descendants and his possessions would be carried off to Babylon and _____ would be left.
$\overline{\hspace{0.4cm}}\overline{\hspace{0.4cm}}\overline{\hspace{0.4cm}}\overline{\hspace{0.4cm}}$
21   32   11   12   34

In this year of the reign of Hezekiah, Sennacherib of Assyria attacked Judah.
$\overline{\hspace{0.4cm}}\overline{\hspace{0.4cm}}\overline{\hspace{0.4cm}}$
33   30   17   36   22   24   19   8

The Lord promised that this city would not be entered by the Assyrians.
$\overline{\hspace{0.4cm}}\overline{\hspace{0.4cm}}\overline{\hspace{0.4cm}}$
27   35   7   25

$\overline{\hspace{0.3cm}}\overline{\hspace{0.3cm}}\overline{\hspace{0.3cm}}\overline{\hspace{0.3cm}}\overline{\hspace{0.3cm}}\overline{\hspace{0.3cm}}\overline{\hspace{0.3cm}}\overline{\hspace{0.3cm}}$
1   2   3   4   5   6   7   8   9   10 11   12 13 14   15 16 17 18 19

20 21   22 23 24   25 26 27 28   29 30 31

32 33   34 35 36 37 38 39.

See 2 Kings 18:5 to check your answer.

Hezekiah

Hezekiah lived at a time when the Israelite tribes were split into two kingdoms. The northern tribes lived in the kingdom of Israel, while the southern tribes lived in the kingdom of Judah. Hezekiah was king of Judah.

Hezekiah's father, Ahaz, had worshipped false gods in the Jerusalem Temple, even sacrificing children to them. Things had gotten worse when Judah's powerful neighbor, Assyria, defeated Judah. The prophet Isaiah told Ahaz that Judah was defeated because it had turned away from God. Hezekiah was completely different from his father. He tore down the false idols, cleaned up the Jerusalem Temple, and invited the northern tribes to a great feast celebrating their dedication to God.

The Assyrians were not happy with Hezekiah's reforms, and they threatened to destroy Jerusalem. Hezekiah wanted to ask Egypt for help in stopping the Assyrians. The prophet Isaiah rejected this plan. The power Judah needed to stop the Assyrians would come from God, not from Egypt's might, Isaiah said. So Hezekiah prayed to God for help. Miraculously, a plague struck the Assyrians' army on its way to Jerusalem, and it turned back without attacking.

REFLECTION

Answer these questions after you have read about Hezekiah.

1. Why does a sports coach or a performance teacher "psyche" you up for a game or recital? Why might you have to psyche yourself up? What is the goal of another team's players or fans when they try to psyche you out?

2. Read 2 Chronicles 32:11–15. Notice the way the Assyrians try to psyche out the people of Jerusalem. What do King Hezekiah and the prophet Isaiah do? How would God help you if you prayed when you felt that someone or something was trying to psyche you out?

Bible Passages about Hezekiah

2 Kings 18:1–8
The nature of Hezekiah's reign

2 Chronicles 29:3–36
Hezekiah purifies
and rededicates the Temple.

2 Kings 18:13–27
Assyrians threaten Jerusalem.

2 Kings 19:1–7
Hezekiah consults with Isaiah.

2 Kings 19:32–37
God conquers the Assyrians.

2 Kings 20:1–11
Hezekiah almost dies
but recovers.

Breakthrough! Articles

Read these articles to learn more about Hezekiah.

***Breakthrough!* Interview with Hezekiah**

One of the Good Guys
2 Kings 18:1–8

Pour Out Your Heart
2 Kings 19:14–19

Josiah

The story of King Josiah is found in 2 Kings 22:1—23:30.
Read the story and complete the following crossword.

ACROSS

1. Josiah was killed in battle against this nation.
5. Josiah removed the priests and destroyed the altars that had been dedicated to false ___.
6. Josiah commanded that all the things used to worship other gods be ___.
8. Josiah stood by a column, or pillar, and made a ___ with the Lord.
9. The high priest Hilkiah found the book of the ___.
10. The book of the Law was ___ before all the people.
12. Mother of Josiah
13. Female prophet who told Josiah that the Lord would punish Jerusalem

DOWN

1. Age of Josiah when he became king
2. Josiah commanded that the people celebrate this.
3. Josiah forbade ___ sacrifice to the god Molech.
4. Josiah lived in this city.
7. The ____ of Josiah succeeded him as ruler of Judah.
8. Josiah's dead body was taken back to Jerusalem in this.
11. Josiah followed the example of this previous king.

Josiah

Josiah was made king of Judah when he was only eight years old, after his father, Amon, was murdered. By this time the kingdom had become very weak—not only politically and militarily, but also in its faithfulness to God. The people worshipped many false gods, and had forgotten the covenant God made with them through Moses.

When he was eighteen, Josiah set about repairing the Jerusalem Temple. A book of Law was discovered during the repairs, possibly the Book of Deuteronomy. After the book was read to him, Josiah realized that his people had broken the covenant. So he destroyed the false idols, had the book of Law read to the people, and brought back the annual celebration of Passover.

Unfortunately, Josiah's reforms came too late. Josiah was killed in a battle against the Egyptians. Not long after, Judah was conquered by the Babylonians. The people were sent into exile, and the Jerusalem Temple was destroyed.

It may seem as if Josiah failed. But although the Temple was destroyed, Josiah had turned many people's hearts back to God. And by reminding his people of the covenant, Josiah gave them a reason for hope during their exile.

REFLECTION

Answer these questions after you have read about Josiah.

1. Though he is the king, King Josiah consults with Hilkiah and Huldah about what to do about significant issues. Name two adults you would approach when facing an important decision. List the personal qualities that make them easy to go to.

2. King Josiah learns that the people of Jerusalem will be severely punished for their years of being unfaithful to God. God has the authority and right to deal punishment when his people disobey. Have you ever learned a lesson from receiving a just punishment? How do people respond when poor leaders create their own rules and punish others unjustly?

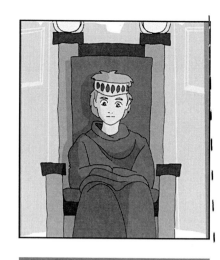

Bible Passages about Josiah

2 Kings 21:23—22:2
Josiah becomes king of Judah at the age of eight.

2 Kings 22:3–20
Josiah consults with Huldah about the Temple book.

2 Kings 23:1–20
Josiah cleanses the Temple and land.

2 Kings 23:21–23
Josiah celebrates a great Passover feast.

2 Kings 23:28–30
Josiah dies.

Breakthrough! Articles

Read these articles to learn more about Josiah.

Breakthrough! Interview with Josiah

An Amazing Woman
2 Kings, chapter 22

A Faith-Filled King
2 Kings 23:1–14

Ezra and Nehemiah

Ezra and Nehemiah were leaders of the Jews after the Exile in Babylon. Each has a book in the Old Testament named for him.

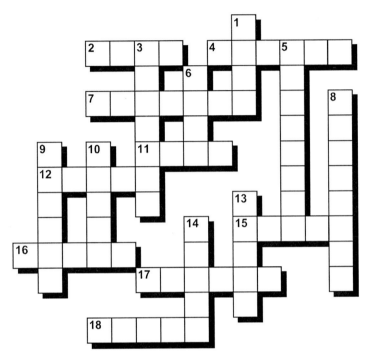

ACROSS

2. Ezra called for the people to _____ and pray for God to protect them. (Ezra 8:21–23)

4. When the Jews returned to Jerusalem from Babylon, they rebuilt the _____. (Ezra 3:8–10)

7. People of the area plotted to fight against the Jews because they did not want them to _____ the city. (Nehemiah 4:1–3)

11. The people answered "_____" to Ezra. (Nehemiah 8:6)

12. The people promised to dedicate the _____ born of each family to God. (Nehemiah 10:36–37)

15. Ezra was a descendant of this high priest. (Ezra 7:1–5)

16. Ezra was unhappy because some of the Jews had foreign _____. (Ezra 9:1–2)

17. When the Jews returned to Jerusalem, they found that the gates of the city had been _____. (Nehemiah 1:1–3)

18. Nehemiah and others worked to rebuild the _____ of the city of Jerusalem. (Nehemiah 2:17)

DOWN

1. Ezra _____ the Law to the people. (Nehemiah 8:1–3)

3. Nehemiah told the people not to work or sell anything on the _____. (Nehemiah 13:15–18)

5. The people began to celebrate this festival again when they returned to Jerusalem. (Ezra 6:19)

6. Nehemiah said he would stand up to his enemies and not _____ in the Temple. (Nehemiah 6:10–11)

8. Nehemiah was _____ of Judah. (Nehemiah 5:14)

9. People living around the Jews tried to make the Jews too _____ to keep building. (Ezra 4:4)

10. Some of the people in the area _____ to complain about the Jews rebuilding the Temple. (Ezra 4:6)

13. Nehemiah ordered the doors to the city _____ shut at the beginning of the Sabbath. (Nehemiah 13:19)

14. This king allowed the Jews in exile to return to Jerusalem. (Ezra 1:1–4)

Ezra and Nehemiah

After the Persians conquered Babylon, the Persian emperor allowed all the Babylonians' foreign captives to return to their homes. When the exiled Israelites returned home, they faced the huge challenge of rebuilding their nation. They had the physical task of rebuilding Jerusalem and its Temple. But they also had the spiritual task of renewing their commitment to their laws and religious practices.

Ezra and Nehemiah were leaders in this rebuilding effort. Ezra was a priest sent by the Persian emperor to Jerusalem with a large group of Israelites. And Nehemiah was made governor of Judah by the emperor.

Besides starting to rebuild Jerusalem and the Temple, Ezra and Nehemiah named scribes and judges to establish law and order. Most important, they rededicated the people to God and the covenant. Ezra read the covenant to the people, and both men emphasized obeying its laws. They urged the Israelites to get rid of everything foreign—starting with their foreign wives. The Babylonians had kept the Israelites prisoners for almost fifty years. Now Ezra and Nehemiah wanted to stop any foreign influences that might keep the nation from becoming strong again.

REFLECTION

Answer these questions after you have read about Ezra and Nehemiah.

1. Ezra and Nehemiah are both involved in rebuilding Jerusalem after its people returned from exile. Think of the people (or yourself, if you were affected) in Joplin, Missouri, whose homes were destroyed by a catastrophic EF-5 tornado in 2011. What do these people need to do to rebuild their town? Are there any people who took on roles similar to Ezra or Nehemiah in the rebuilding? What challenges did they face?

2. Ezra and Nehemiah spoke out against marriages to foreign people. They feared that in those marriages the Jewish spouse would lose his or her religious faith and traditions. Which aspects of your own ethnic and religious background do you want to be sure not to lose?

Bible Passages about Ezra and Nehemiah

Ezra 1:1–10
Ezra's time: Cyrus sends the Jews back to Jerusalem.

Ezra 7:1–10
Ezra's background

Ezra 9:1—10:17
Ezra leads people in denouncing mixed marriages.

Nehemiah, chapters 1–2
Nehemiah returns to Judah to help rebuild Jerusalem.

Nehemiah 10:28–39
The people of Jerusalem promise to reform.

Nehemiah, chapter 13
Nehemiah reforms the people of Jerusalem.

Breakthrough! Articles

Read these articles to learn more about Ezra and Nehemiah.

Breakthrough! Interview with Ezra and Nehemiah

Introduction to the Books of Ezra and Nehemiah

Answers to Prayer
Ezra 7:27–28

Mixed Marriages
Ezra, chapters 9–10

Big Deal, a Wall
Nehemiah, chapters 2–3

Nehemiah Works for Justice
Nehemiah 5:1–13

The Dedication
Nehemiah 12:27–43

Judith

Judith is a biblical heroine because she saved her people from destruction. Put the events of Judith's life in the correct order of how they happened. You can figure this out by scanning the headlines in the Book of Judith. Number the events 1 through 18 in the spaces provided. Starting with event number 1, write the bold, underlined letters in the spaces provided at the bottom. Some events have two letters in bold, underlined type. Be sure to put those letters in the spaces in the order in which they appear in the sentence.

1. _____ Achior is taken by the Assyrians to the town of Bethulia and left there.

2. _____ Achior says that the Israelites of Judah cannot be defeated if they are faithful to God.

3. _____ Holofernes announces that he and the army of his king can defeat the Jews and their God.

4. _____ Holofernes holds a war council to decide how to deal with the Israelites.

5. _____ Holofernes is tricked into thinking Judith will help him defeat the Israelites.

6. _____ Holofernes lays siege to Bethulia and blocks sources of food and water.

7. _____ Holofernes wages war on the nations in the west.

8. _____ Judith chops off the head of the drunk Holofernes.

9. _____ Judith goes to the camp of Holofernes.

10. _____ Judith meets with the town officials and tells them not to test the Lord.

11. _____ Judith returned to Bethulia and showed off Holofernes' head.

12. _____ Judith sings a hymn of praise.

13. _____ The king of Assyria decides to conquer the nations in the west that would not be his allies.

14. _____ The Israelites attacked the leaderless Assyrian army.

15. _____ The Israelites of Judah (Judea) plan to defend themselves against Holofernes.

16. _____ The Israelites pray to God to protect them.

17. _____ The people of Bethulia, weak and dying, tell their leaders to give up.

18. _____ War breaks out between the Assyrians and the Medes.

___ ___ ___ ___ ___ ___ ___ ___ ___ ___ ___ ___

___ ___ ___ ___ ___ ___ ___ ___ ___ ___ ___.

Judith

As the Book of Judith opens, the powerful Assyrian army is on the march against Jerusalem. All that stands in its way is the town of Bethulia, whose leaders are about to surrender.

Even though the men of Bethulia want to surrender, a childless widow named Judith says that she will stop the Assyrians with God's help. After praying, she dresses as beautifully as possible and, with her maid, goes down to the Assyrian camp.

The Assyrians take her to their general, Holofernes, who is amazed by Judith's beauty. She tells the general that she is sure he will defeat the Jews, and she promises to show him a way to win the battle without losing a single soldier.

Pleased, Holofernes makes Judith and her maid welcome in the camp. He even invites her to dinner with him alone in his tent. After drinking too much, he passes out. After saying a prayer, Judith takes his sword, cuts off his head, and places it in a sack. Then she and her maid sneak out of the camp.

The Assyrians panic when they discover what has happened the next morning, and the Jews chase them down as they flee. In her victory song, Judith praises God for doing great things through those who have faith in him.

REFLECTION

Answer these questions after you have read about Judith.

1. Although Judith is a wealthy woman, she puts God above all else. What are some things or activities or people that Christians can put before God? Ask God for help to put your own priorities in proper order.

2. Judith and her maid showed great bravery in going into the enemy's camp. They were able to overcome any fear because of their trust in God. When and where are you called to be brave? How is your trust in God connected with overcoming your fears?

3. Judith prays before, during, and after her encounter with Holofernes. Why is it important for today's military officers to pray regularly? Why is it also important that soldiers have access to chaplains while they are preparing for and engaging in military action?

Bible Passages about Judith

Judith 8:1–8
Description of Judith

Judith 8:9–36
Judith challenges the plan of the Israelite elders.

Judith, chapter 9
Judith prays to God for assistance.

Judith 10:6—13:11
Judith goes to the Assyrians and meets Holofernes.

Judith 13:12–20
Israel praises God and Judith.

Judith 14—15:7
Israelites defeats the Assyrians.

Judith 15:8–13
Israelites praise Judith.

Breakthrough! Articles

Read these articles to learn more about Judith.

Breakthrough! Interview with Judith

Peace, Not Violence
Judith 13:1–10

Esther

Esther is a biblical heroine because she saved her people from destruction. Put the events of Esther's life in the correct order of how they happened. You can figure this out by scanning the headlines in the Book of Esther. Number the events 1 through 14 in the spaces provided. Starting with event number 1, write the bold, underlined letters in the spaces provided at the bottom of the page.

1. _____ Esther goes before <u>t</u>he king.

2. _____ Esther invites the king and Haman <u>to</u> a banquet for the first time.

3. _____ Esther is chosen as qu<u>e</u>en.

4. _____ Esther prays and fast<u>s</u> to get courage.

5. _____ Haman plots with his wi<u>f</u>e to kill Mordecai.

6. _____ Haman is hanged on the gallows, or gibbet, he bui<u>l</u>t for Mordecai.

7. _____ Haman plans to kill all the Jews o<u>f</u> the empire because Mordecai, a Jew, will not bow down to Haman, but only to God.

8. _____ Mordec<u>a</u>i tells Esther she must talk with the king about the king's decree.

9. _____ Mordecai, cousin and guardian of Es<u>t</u>her, dreams about dragons ready to fight.

10. _____ The festival of Purim is e<u>s</u>tablished.

11. _____ The Jews destroy <u>t</u>heir enemies.

12. _____ The king issues a decree in fav<u>o</u>r of the Jews.

13. _____ The king sends out a proclamation that says all Jews will be killed in one day.

14. _____ Queen Vashti refuses to appear before t<u>he</u> king.

The feast of Purim is also called

__ __ __ __ __ __ __ __

__ __ __ __ __ __.

Esther

Esther's dramatic story begins when the king of Persia dismisses his queen for not coming when he calls her. Then he searches among all the beautiful young women in the land for one to be his new queen. He chooses Esther, an orphan who was raised by her cousin, Mordecai. Esther is a Jew, but Mordecai tells her to keep her religion a secret.

One day Mordecai refuses to bow before one of the king's officials. That official, Haman, gets his revenge by tricking the king into ordering that all the Jews be killed on a certain date.

When Mordecai hears about this, he asks Queen Esther to talk to the king. But anyone who approaches the king without first being called by him is to be put to death, unless the king holds out his scepter. Esther fasts and prays for three days. When she finally approaches the king, he holds out his scepter and offers to grant her any wish. Esther invites the king and Haman to two banquets. During the second banquet, she begs for her own life and the lives of her people, and explains Haman's plot. The king has Haman killed, and issues an order allowing the Jews to kill anyone who tries to harm them. The Jews celebrate this with a great feast, called Purim, which is celebrated every year by Jews even today.

REFLECTION

Answer these questions after you have read about Esther.

1. Read Mordecai's and Esther's prayer in chapter C. What does it mean to trust God? What does praying have to do with having trust in God?

2. Esther and Mordecai do not intend to become heroes. Instead, the circumstances force them to choose that role or to let evil happen. If you found yourself in their situation, what would you do? Can you tell about a time when you had to trust in God during a difficult situation?

Bible Passages about Esther

Esther, chapters A and 1
Mordecai's rise; Queen Vashti's departure

Esther 2:1–18
Esther becomes queen.

Esther 2:19–23, chapters B and 3
Haman and the king plot to kill the Jews.

Esther, chapters 4 and C
Esther's prayerful plea

Esther, chapters D and 5–7
Esther's banquet

Esther, chapters 8, E, and 9
Esther and Mordecai save the Jews.

Breakthrough! Articles

Read these articles to learn more about Esther.

Supporting Immigrants
Esther 2:10–11

The Final Solution
Esther, chapter 3

Let Nothing Disturb You
Esther C:23–25

The Courage of a Queen
Esther 4:9–17, D:1–16

Saving the Jews
Esther 8:1–12

The Festival of Purim
Esther 9:20–31

Name: _____

The Maccabees

The Maccabean Revolt is named for the nickname of one of its heroes, Judas Maccabeus. Maccabeus means "hammer," and Judas was a ferocious fighter. His father, his five brothers, and Judas led the Jews in a war for religious and political freedom from their cruel Greek rulers. All passages below are from 1 Maccabees.

1. **M** _ _ _ _ _ _ _ _ _
2. _ _ _ **A** _
3. _ _ _ _ _ **C** _ _ _
4. _ _ _ _ _ _ **C** _ _ _ _
5. _ _ _ **A** _ _ _
6. **B** _ _ _
7. _ _ _ **E**
8. _ _ _ _ _ **E** _
9. **S** _ _ _ _

1. This priest sparked the beginning of the revolt. (2:15–28)

2. He took command after his father died. (3:1–2)

3. This king was furious with the Jewish revolt and put together a large army to fight the Jews. (3:27–28)

4. Judas and his men secured Jerusalem and purified the Temple and _____ the altar (sanctuary). (4:36–61)

5. This son of Mattathias sacrificed his life in the revolt. (6:32–46)

6. Nicanor led his army to Jerusalem and threatened to _____ the Temple. (7:26–38)

7. Judas and the Jews made an alliance, or treaty, with _____. (8:1–22)

8. Trypho killed Jonathan and sent troops here to kill his soldiers. (12:39–53)

9. This brother took over and finally succeeded in winning the revolt. (13:15–16)

Read 1 Maccabees 13:31–42. In what year did the Jews win their battle for freedom?

_____

Checking the footnotes of your Bible, what year is that in the current calendar?

_____

The Maccabees

The Israelites lived under the foreign rule of the Babylonians, Persians, and Greeks for nearly five hundred years. For the most part, they submitted to this rule. But then one of the Greek rulers started forcing everyone in his empire to adopt Greek culture—including the worship of Greek gods. He outlawed the Israelites' religious practices, and put a statue of the Greek god Zeus in the Jerusalem Temple.

One day a Greek official tried to force a priest named Mattathias to offer a sacrifice to a pagan god. Instead, Mattathias killed the Greek, starting a revolt that was led by his five sons. They became known as the Maccabees, a word that means "hammer," because their attacks were like hammer blows. They fought the Greeks for more than twenty years and finally won.

One of the stories from this time is about the faith of a mother and her seven sons who were arrested and tortured to force them to break God's Law. When they refused, they were put to death, one by one. They went to their deaths telling the king that although he was taking their lives, God would raise them up again to live forever. Their response shows their belief in God's final victory over death.

REFLECTION

Answer these questions after you have read about the Maccabees.

1. The Maccabees resist the Greeks, who want to impose their religious beliefs on them and other Jews. There is a parallel between imposing beliefs through military might and imposing beliefs through peer pressure. When someone tries to make fun of you or others because of religious beliefs, family, clothing, or appearance, what can you learn from the Maccabees about your own dignity and rights? Where did the Maccabees get their strength? How can you rely on this same strength?

2. When Mattathias decides to resist the oppressors, the Greeks, his whole family supports him. When does your family band together? What can we learn from the Maccabees about being a family?

Bible Passages about the Maccabees

1 Maccabees 1:20–53
Antiochus persecutes Jews.

1 Maccabees 2:15–28
Mattathias refuses to submit to Greeks.

**1 Maccabees 3:1–9,
2 Maccabees 8:1–7**
Judas leads victories against enemies.

**1 Maccabees 4:36–59,
2 Maccabees 10:1–8**
Purification and rededication of the Temple

2 Maccabees 12:38–45
Judas encourages soldiers to pray for their deceased comrades.

Breakthrough! Articles

Read these articles to learn more about the Maccabees.

Introduction to the First Book of the Maccabees

Introduction to the Second Book of the Maccabees

Breakthrough! **Interview with the Maccabees**

Hanukkah
2 Maccabees 2:16–18

Integrity
2 Maccabees 6:18–31

Prayer for Protection
2 Maccabees 10:25–26

Job

The Book of Job explores the question of why bad things happen to good people. Job is a good man whose faith is tested by terrible things. His friends come to him and tell him that he must have done something wrong. Job answers that he has not; he has always done what was right. Read the passages indicated and unscramble the words according to your reading. Then write the numbered letters in the proper spaces at the bottom of the page to complete the sentence there. All passages are found in the Book of Job.

God allows him to test Job. (1:6–12)
N A S T A

___ ___ ___ ___ ___
    4   10 11

Job loses his ____ and his workers. (1:13–17)
M A S N I L A

___ ___ ___ ___ ___ ___ ___
  12   3 22

Job's _____ die. (1:18–19)
N E L H I R C D

___ ___ ___ ___ ___ ___ ___ ___
  1   19 18 23

Job's wife tells him to curse ___ and die. (2:9)
D G O

___ ___ ___
25   17

Eliphaz tells Job that we bring these on ourselves. (5:6–7)
R O T S E U B L

___ ___ ___ ___ ___ ___ ___
14   13 15

Bildad tells Job that his children must have done this. (8:3–4)
N I E N S D

___ ___ ___ ___ ___ ___
     7 16   27

Zophar tells Job that he must have done something wrong and that he should set his ____ right. (11:13–14)
E R T A H

___ ___ ___ ___ ___
     6   21

Eliphaz tells Job that he must be guilty and his own words ____ him. (15:6)
C O N N E M D

___ ___ ___ ___ ___ ___ ___
  26   24   5

Zophar tells Job that this kind of people suffer. (20:12–19)
W I D K E C

___ ___ ___ ___ ___ ___
9   8

Job answers them that he is a ___ man. (29:14)
S J T U

___ ___ ___ ___
  2 20

In Job, chapters 38–42, the Lord answers Job and tells him that Job is

___ ___ ___ ___ ___   ___ ___ ___   ___ ___ ___ ___ ___ ___
1 2 3 4 5   6 7 8   9 10 11 12 13 14

___ ___ ___ ___ ___ ___ ___ ___ ___ ___   ___ ___ ___.
15 16 17 18 19 20 21 22 23 24   25 26 27

Job

Most Israelites believed that God rewarded good people and punished bad people. When people suffered, it was assumed to be God's punishment for some sin. The author of the Book of Job didn't completely agree with this belief; after all, bad things sometimes happen to very good people.

In the story, Job is a perfectly holy man who has been blessed with great wealth, a large family, and good health. Up in Heaven, however, Satan tells God that Job will be holy only as long as his life is good. As soon as Job suffers, Satan says, Job will curse God.

So God allows Job to lose everything. His animals and servants are stolen or killed. His children are killed in a storm. His wife tells him to curse God for allowing these bad things to happen. Job refuses to do this, but he does question why God would allow an innocent person to suffer. His friends say it must be because he sinned, but Job knows he is innocent, and he demands an explanation from God.

Finally, God appears to Job and quizzes him about the mysteries of creation, all of which Job admits he does not understand. How then, God asks, can Job expect to understand the mystery of suffering? In the face of this mystery, the Book of Job says, the best humans can do is to stay faithful to God.

REFLECTION

Answer these questions after you have read about Job.

1. Job suffers quite a bit because of Satan, but Job continues to be faithful to God. Has suffering ever tempted you to lose faith? How do the people you know deal with difficulties and suffering?

2. Job's situation is very bad (Job 2:7–9). Where do you see people in situations like Job's today? What could you do to help someone in this type of situation?

3. Job's three friends came and sat silently with him for seven days and nights because of his suffering (Job 2:13). They knew this was the best way to support Job. Do you have someone in your life who can read your moods and know how to respond effectively to them? Can you strengthen your own skills to be supportive of others?

Bible Passages about Job

Job 1:1–12
Job's goodness; God accepts Satan's bet.

Job 1:13–22
Job loses everything.

Job 2:1–10
Satan gives Job sores, but he remains faithful.

Job, chapters 29–31
Job pleads his cause and maintains his innocence.

Job, chapters 38–41
The Lord answers Job.

Job, chapter 42
Job answers the Lord and has his life restored.

Breakthrough! Articles

Read these articles to learn more about Job.

***Breakthrough!* Interview with Job**

The Fall from a Good Life
Job, chapter 1

Being There Is Enough
Job 2:11–13

Integrity
Job 27:1–6

Keepin' an Eye Out
Job 29:2–5

God's Wisdom
Job 40:1–5

God's Blessing for Job
Job, chapter 42

Lady Wisdom

Lady Wisdom is a name we use for the way some ancient Israelites talked about the wisdom of God. The Books of Proverbs, Wisdom, Sirach, and the Song of Songs describe wisdom as a woman. Wisdom is the ability to make good judgments. A wise person is not necessarily the most intelligent or the most educated person, but someone who knows how to use the knowledge he or she has. Read the passages below and then cut out and rearrange the boxes to learn about Lady Wisdom.

In Wisdom 6:17, we learn that:

BE	WE	LE	SI	WIS	DOM	Y W	ARN

NCE	HEN	S W	REL	ANT	TO	GIN

In Wisdom 7:24, we learn that:

S E	THA	YTH	VER	IS	ING	SO	T S

ATE	PU	HE	PEN	RE	DOM	WIS	ETR

In Wisdom 7:9, we learn that:

BE	OM	WHA	VER	GET	FR	WIS	IS

T Y	DOM	OU	SIL	R T	GO	OR	LD

HAN	TTE

In Wisdom 10:9, we learn that:

ES	FRO	DOM	SCU	M D	WIS	RE	ER

ANG	US

Lady Wisdom

Some of the Bible's books—the Book of Proverbs, the Book of Wisdom, the Book of Sirach, the Song of Songs—use the image of a woman to praise the goodness of wisdom. According to the Bible, wisdom is not the same as intelligence or knowledge; rather, it is the ability to make good decisions, especially in choosing between right and wrong. The Bible presents wisdom as one of the most valuable virtues a person can have. When God told King Solomon to ask for anything he wanted, the king asked for wisdom rather than riches or a long life.

The Bible uses the image of a perfect woman to describe the attractiveness of wisdom. In one place the Book of Wisdom says her beauty is more radiant than the sun and stars (Wisdom 7:29). Who wouldn't want to get to know her? And yet the Bible presents another woman who competes with Wisdom for people's hearts: Folly. Both Wisdom and Folly (foolishness) are beautiful, but Folly leads her followers into ruin, while Wisdom leads her followers to God.

REFLECTION

Answer these questions after you have read about Lady Wisdom.

1. Skim through the Book of Proverbs, chapters 10–22. When you find a passage that strikes you as being especially wise, stop your search. Then think of a creative way you could convey this wisdom on a billboard—in a way that would catch people's attention but not preach at them. Draw a sketch of this billboard below.

2. Think for a bit about wisdom you have learned in your life. Examples of wisdom include your own insights, something you read, thoughts shared by your parents or a teacher, proverbs, teachings of Jesus, and so on. Write down five pieces of wisdom that you think about and apply in your life fairly regularly. Ask yourself, is this wisdom a gift from God?

Bible Passages about Lady Wisdom

Proverbs 1:20–33
Wisdom reprimands those who ignore her.

Proverbs, chapter 8
Wisdom describes herself.

Wisdom 6:12–21
The value of Wisdom is explained.

Wisdom 8:2–20
Solomon declares his love for Wisdom.

Sirach 24:1–29
Wisdom recounts her role in the history of Israel.

Breakthrough! Articles

Read these articles to learn more about lady Wisdom.

Breakthrough! **Interview with Lady Wisdom**

Introduction to Job, Psalms, Proverbs, Song of Songs, Wisdom, Sirach

God's Wisdom
Job 40:1–5

Two Ways
Proverbs 4:24–27

A Great Gift!
Song of Songs 6:1–9

The Gift of Wisdom
Wisdom 7:22—8:1

Don't Judge a Book . . .
Sirach 11:2–6

Name: _____

Isaiah

The Book of Isaiah covers several hundred years in the history of Israel. It also records the preaching of several prophets. In it the prophets speak of the sins of the people, the coming fall of the nation and the Exile, and the future of the people of God.

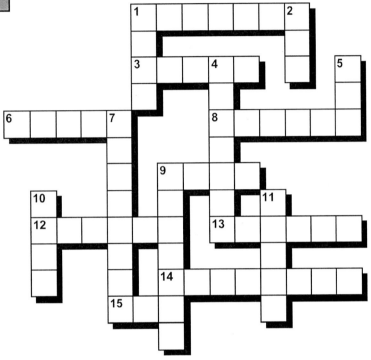

ACROSS

1. Isaiah said the ___ were misleading the people. (Isaiah 3:12)
3. Isaiah told of a child who would be born and would be called the Prince of ___. (Isaiah 9:5–6)
6. Isaiah spoke of new heavens and the new ___. (Isaiah 66:22)
8. God's love is compared to the love of a ___. (Isaiah 49:14–15)
9. Isaiah told the people that offering ___ to the hungry pleases God. (Isaiah 58:10)
12. Those who trust in the Lord and wait for him to save them will be taken up on ___ wings. (Isaiah 40:31)
13. The Lord appeared on a ___ to Isaiah. (Isaiah 6:1)
14. Isaiah told of a woman who would have a child and name him ___. (Isaiah 7:14)
15. The name of Isaiah's ___ was a prediction of what was to happen to Samaria. (Isaiah 8:3–4)

DOWN

1. An angel touched Isaiah's ___ with a burning coal or ember. (Isaiah 6:6–7)
2. In a vision, Isaiah saw flaming creatures with this number of wings. (Isaiah 6:2)
4. God told Isaiah to ___ his people. (Isaiah 40:1)
5. Isaiah said there would come a time when nations would no longer go to ___. (Isaiah 2:4)
7. Isaiah preached that God wanted the people to help the ___. (Isaiah 58:7)
9. Isaiah told the people what true ___ is. (Isaiah 58:1–7)
10. Isaiah replied to the Lord, "___ me!" (Isaiah 6:8)
11. Isaiah accused the people of spending time getting ___. (Isaiah 5:11)

Isaiah

Isaiah began his career as a prophet after experiencing a powerful vision of God in the Temple. That vision inspired his total trust in God. He advised the kings of Judah to trust God's power too. Some of Judah's kings sought protection from their enemies by making treaties with foreign nations.

Although Isaiah respected the kings, he was well aware of their failings. He criticized the way the rich ruling class treated the poor, and predicted the coming of a perfect ruler—later known as the Messiah—who would bring justice and peace to everyone.

A long time after Isaiah died, the kingdom of Judah was destroyed by Babylon, and its people sent into exile or slavery there. Another prophet came along to comfort the people in exile. Using Isaiah's name and ideas, this Second Isaiah described a servant of God whose suffering is used to fulfill God's plan. Just as God does not abandon the servant, Second Isaiah promises the people that God will rescue them from their suffering too.

A third prophet (again using Isaiah's name) celebrated this rescue when the Exile ended after about fifty years. He urged the people to practice justice toward one another, and predicted the coming of a perfect kingdom.

REFLECTION

Answer these questions after you have read about Isaiah.

1. The role of the prophet can be likened to the role of a sports coach. Both are involved in trying to motivate the people they are in charge of to "play up to their ability" by using a combination of warnings and encouragements. From your experience of having coaches or seeing coaches in action, what personal qualities do you think a successful prophet would have?

2. Go into a dark room where you also have a candle or flashlight. Sit in the dark for a few minutes. Why do you think Isaiah uses the image of the dark to describe people who are in trouble, without God? Light the candle or turn on the flashlight and observe the way light floods the room. How does God's presence chase away darkness?

Bible Passages about Isaiah

Isaiah 2:1–5
Isaiah predicts future peace to Jerusalem.

Isaiah 6:1–8
God calls Isaiah.

Isaiah 44:1–3
God consoles Israel.

Isaiah 49:1–6
Israel is a light to the nations.

Isaiah 52:13—53:12
The Suffering Servant

Isaiah 65:17–25
Isaiah predicts a new Heaven, a new earth, and a new Jerusalem.

Breakthrough! Articles

Read these articles to learn more about Isaiah.

Prophets and Prophecy
Isaiah, chapter 6

Names of God
Isaiah 9:6

A New Section
Isaiah, chapter 40

The Suffering Servant
Isaiah 49:1–6

Beautiful Feet?
Isaiah, chapter 52

Help from the Holy Trinity
Isaiah 65:17–25

Name: _____

Jeremiah

Jeremiah was a prophet to Judah whose life was a symbol for the sorrows of Judah. Read the indicated passages from the Book of Jeremiah to complete the statements below. To find out if your answers are correct, check for each of your answers in the word search. Write the unused letters from the word search in the spaces at the bottom of the page to spell out a fact about Jeremiah.

1. Jeremiah said he was a boy and too __ __ __ __ __ to speak for God. (Jeremiah 1:6)

2. Enemies of Jeremiah called for his __ __ __ __ __. (Jeremiah 26:7–8)

3. Jeremiah could not find even __ __ __ honest, just, or upright person in Jerusalem. (Jeremiah 5:1–5)

4. God told Jeremiah to __ __ __ __ __ a jar (jug or flask) to show what will happen to the people. (Jeremiah 19:1–6,10–11)

5. When the __ __ __ __ __ __, Pashur, heard Jeremiah preaching, he had him beaten and put in chains. (Jeremiah 20:1–2)

6. Jeremiah felt a __ __ __ __ burning in his heart to preach the Word of the Lord. (Jeremiah 20:9)

7. Jeremiah wrote a __ __ __ __ __ __ to the exiles in Babylon. (Jeremiah 29:1–14)

8. Jeremiah spoke of a new _____ that God would make with Israel. (Jeremiah 31:31)

9. God told Jeremiah that he was called to be a __ __ __ __ __ __ __ before he was even born. (Jeremiah 1:5)

10. Jeremiah was __ __ __ __ __ __ __ __ __ __ because someone thought he was deserting to the enemy. (Jeremiah 37:11–16)

J	E	R	E	M	I	A	H	H	I
G	N	U	O	Y	P	T	W	M	T
A	S	F	O	R	A	E	P	B	N
R	C	E	I	E	D	R	E	R	A
T	O	E	D	F	I	I	N	E	N
L	S	E	E	S	T	F	O	A	E
T	P	R	O	P	H	E	T	K	V
O	E	N	R	E	T	T	E	L	O
G	E	Y	P	T	+	+	+	+	C
D	+	+	+	+	+	+	+	+	+

__ __ __ __ __ __ __ __ __

__ __ __ __ __ __ __ __ __ __ __

__ __ __ __ __ __ __ __ __.

Jeremiah

Jeremiah was something of a reluctant prophet; when God called him, Jeremiah said that he was too young to speak for God. But God would not take no for an answer.

Jeremiah began his work when King Josiah ruled Judah. Josiah was a good king and encouraged the people to obey their covenant with God. But Jeremiah feared Josiah's changes came too late to save Judah from destruction. After Josiah died the next kings were corrupt and did not continue Josiah's religious reforms. Jeremiah criticized these kings, and warned of Judah's coming destruction. Some people thought God would protect Jerusalem because the Temple was there. These people were mistaken, Jeremiah said, because the people had broken the covenant. Speaking this message got Jeremiah jailed, beaten, and thrown into a well and left to die.

Judah eventually did fall to the invading Babylonians. The Babylonians destroyed the Temple and sent most of the survivors as prisoners to Babylon. After this Jeremiah offered hope by predicting that Babylon would be destroyed, and that the people would be free to return to Judah. Then, Jeremiah said, God would make a New Covenant with the people, one that would live in their hearts.

REFLECTION

Answer these questions after you have read about Jeremiah.

1. Read about God's call to Jeremiah in Jeremiah 1:1–10. Jeremiah, like many young people, feels uncomfortable speaking out on a topic, especially in front of adults. Notice, however, that when God calls young people to do his work, God also gives them the power to do so. What work do you think God is calling you to do right now?

2. Our world is very different from Jeremiah's. We have cell phones, the Internet, cable TV, and world news at our fingertips. Yet it is usually not people like Jeremiah who make the news. Are there prophets out there saying important things that do not make the news? If so, can you describe any of them and what they might be saying?

Bible Passages about Jeremiah

Jeremiah 1:1–10
God calls Jeremiah.

Jeremiah 4:1–31
The coming destruction

Jeremiah 15:10–21, 18:18–23, 20:7–18
Jeremiah argues with God.

Jeremiah 18:1–12
Jeremiah goes to a potter's house.

Jeremiah 31:1–14, 31–40
God tells Jeremiah of the New Covenant.

Jeremiah 37:1—38:13
Jeremiah is imprisoned.

Breakthrough! Articles

Read these articles to learn more about Jeremiah.

Who, Me?
Jeremiah 1:4–10

Help! Rescue Me!
Jeremiah 2:26–27

Why Me, O Lord?
Jeremiah 15:10–21

My Place of Safety
Jeremiah 17:14–18

Falsely Accused
Jeremiah, chapter 26

Down and Out
Jeremiah 38:1–13

Ezekiel

The prophet Ezekiel had many visions as he preached to the people of Judah. Read the passages for each statement below from Ezekiel, and then complete the statement. To find out if your answers are correct, check for each of your answers in the word search. Write the unused letters from the word search in the spaces at the bottom of the page to spell out a fact about Ezekiel.

1. Ezekiel was among the ___ at the River Chebar. (6 letters) (Ezekiel 1:1)

2. Ezekiel saw ___ in a vision. (6 letters) (Ezekiel 1:15–21)

3. Ezekiel was told in one of his visions to eat a ___. (6 letters) (Ezekiel 2:1–10)

4. To symbolize the sins of Israel, God told Ezekiel to build a miniature of Jerusalem and lie on his ___. (4 letters) (Ezekiel 4:1–8)

5. Ezekiel was to cut his ___ and scatter it in the miniature city he made. (4 letters) (Ezekiel 5:1–4)

6. God showed Ezekiel a ___ in a wall that led to the Temple. (4 letters) (Ezekiel 8:7)

7. In one of his visions, Ezekiel saw the ___ of God leaving the Temple in Jerusalem. (5 letters) (Ezekiel 10:15–18)

8. God promised to establish an everlasting ___ with Israel. (8 letters) (Ezekiel 16:59–60)

E	Z	E	K	I	T	S	C	R	O	L	L
E	L	W	A	S	N	A	P	R	G	E	O
J	E	R	U	S	A	L	E	M	L	V	P
H	E	T	T	S	N	O	J	U	O	I	D
A	H	A	S	N	E	D	W	A	R	L	S
T	H	O	L	E	V	N	A	K	Y	E	N
I	N	T	E	O	O	E	O	H	A	I	R
E	X	I	E	L	C	E	X	B	I	N	B
D	R	E	H	P	E	H	S	I	Y	A	B
Y	L	O	W	N	+	+	I	+	L	R	+
E	L	P	M	E	T	+	D	+	+	E	D
+	+	+	+	+	+	+	E	+	+	+	S

9. God told Ezekiel that he wanted Israel to change its ___ ways. (4 letters) (Ezekiel 33:10–11)

10. Ezekiel learned of the fall of the city of ___. (9 letters) (Ezekiel 33:21)

11. In one of Ezekiel's visions, God compared himself to a ___. (8 letters) (Ezekiel 34:11–16)

12. Ezekiel saw a vision of ___ that came to life. (8 letters) (2 words) (Ezekiel 37:1–14)

13. Ezekiel had a vision of a new ___. (6 letters) (Ezekiel 40:1–7)

___ ___ ___ ___ ___ ___   ___ ___ ___   ___

___ ___ ___ ___ ___ ___ ___ ___   ___ ___ ___ ___   ___

___ ___ ___   ___ ___ ___ ___ ___ ___ ___ ___

___ ___ ___ ___ ___ ___ ___ ___ ___ ___

___ ___   ___ ___ ___ ___ ___ ___ ___ .

Ezekiel

Ezekiel was a priest who became a prophet after he had a fantastic vision of God. The Israelites had become so corrupt, according to Ezekiel's vision, that God had abandoned the Temple. This would have been a shocking message for most Israelites. They believed they would be safe as long as God's presence remained with them in the Temple. Ezekiel's hard message was that sin has serious consequences.

Ezekiel had a unique way of getting his message across: he acted it out, often in bizarre, attention-getting ways. For example, God made him speechless for a while to represent the Israelites' refusal to listen to God. Another time he shaved his head and beard—just as slaves and prisoners were forced to do—and burned the hair as a sign of the hardships the Israelites would experience.

After the Babylonians destroyed the Temple and forced the Israelite survivors into slavery in Babylon, Ezekiel's message became one of hope. He described a vision in which dead bones were brought to life—a sign of how God would restore Israel. And, like Jeremiah, he predicted that God would write a New Covenant on their hearts.

REFLECTION

Answer these questions after you have read about Ezekiel.

1. God tells Ezekiel that his life as a prophet will be like this: "They will defy and despise you; it will be like living among scorpions. Still, don't be afraid of those rebels" (Ezekiel 2:6). Knowing this, why would Ezekiel accept the call to be a prophet? Why do some people attack other people who are only trying to be faithful to God?

2. Ezekiel's prophecy communicates that actions have consequences, but that God gives second chances for poor choices. Why is it good to know that your choices have consequences for you and others? How are moral guidelines connected to the consequences of your choices?

Bible Passages about Ezekiel

Ezekiel 1:1–28
Ezekiel sees God's throne.

Ezekiel 2:1–10
God calls Ezekiel.

Ezekiel 3:1–15
Ezekiel eats the scroll and receives the spirit.

Ezekiel 34:11–31
God as the good shepherd

Ezekiel 36:22–36
God will give the people a new heart and mind.

Ezekiel 37:1–14
Vision of the dry bones

Breakthrough! Articles

Read these articles to learn more about Ezekial.

Breakthrough! Interview with Ezekiel

Introduction to the Book of Ezekiel

Only God Is God
Ezekiel, chapters 2–3

I.M.s from God?
Ezekiel 4:1—5:4

God Is . . .
Ezekiel 10:4

Praying with New Life
Ezekiel, chapter 37

Name: _____

Hosea

Hosea was a prophet to the northern kingdom of Israel. Hosea used his own unhappy marriage to a prostitute to describe the relationship between Israel and God. Read Hosea, chapters 1–3. Then cut out and rearrange the boxes to learn about the message of Hosea.

In chapter 1, we learn that:

IM	HFU	HOS	RIE	WO	MED	O H	D A
O W	AS	WH	MER	AIT	MAN	GO	NA
L T	UNF	EA	MAR				

In chapter 2, we learn that:

AS	HFU	WA	ISR	OME	AEL	L T	GO
FUL	UNF	AIT	O H	R W	TO	NFA	D A
ITH	S U	A	OSE	S G			

In chapters 2 and 3, we learn that:

T A	OD	F G	THE	IFE	RAE	EA	TAN
HOS	VE	S A	E O	LO	IS	HE	S W
WA	S C	OF	LOV	FOR	FOR	S T	L
ONS	HI						

81

Hosea

Hosea was a prophet who lived in the northern kingdom of Israel. God told Hosea to marry the prostitute Gomer. Together they had three children. The children's names reveal Hosea's heartache to come. The first son was named Jezreel, symbolizing God's punishment for the murders done in that city; his daughter was named Loruhamah, meaning "unloved"; and his second son was named Lo-ammi, meaning "not my people."

Hosea's love for his wife was a symbol for the love God had for Israel. Just as Hosea's wife had betrayed him by being with other men, the people of Israel betrayed God by worshipping other gods. Gomer became the symbol for Israel's shame.

But Hosea's message was that if the people gave up their evil ways and returned to God, God would save them again. Just as Hosea loved his unfaithful wife and kept accepting her back, God would also take back the people of Israel. Hosea used the image of his own love for his unfaithful wife to remind the people of God's everlasting love for them, despite their unfaithfulness.

Bible Passages about Hosea

Hosea 1:1–9
Hosea obeys God's request to marry Gomer.

Hosea 1:10—3:5
Consequences for an unfaithful wife

Hosea, chapter 3
Hosea and God are both faithful.

Hosea, chapter 11
God's tender love for his children

Hosea 12:1—14:3
The consequences of Israel's unfaithfulness

Hosea 14:4–9
God promises new life.

REFLECTION

Answer these questions after you have read about Hosea.

1. Imagine that God is saying these things to you and the people in your parish or church. Fill in the blanks:

    "But the LORD says, '_____ (name of your parish), what am I going to do with you? Your love for me disappears as quickly as _____ ; it is like _____, that vanishes. . . . That is why I have sent my prophets to you with my message of _____ . What I want from you is plain and clear: I want your constant love, not your _____. I would rather have my people know me than _____ to me'." (Adapted from Hosea 6:4–6)

    Why did you fill it in as you did?

2. Hosea uses some interesting descriptions for problems in his day. (See Hosea 4:16, 7:8, 7:16.) What type of expression would you use to describe a problem in society today? Why did you choose this expression?

***Breakthrough!* Articles**

Read these articles to learn more about Hosea.

***Breakthrough!* Interview with Hosea**

Introduction to the Book of Hosea

Name: _____

Amos

Amos was a prophet to Israel who accused the people of sins and warned them of their coming destruction by Assyria.

ACROSS

1. The Lord showed Amos a vision of ___ and spoke of the destruction of Israel. (Amos 7:1–3)

3. Amos called for ___ to flow like water. (Amos 5:24)

5. The Lord showed Amos a vision of ___ and spoke of the destruction of Israel. (Amos 7:4–6)

6. Hometown of Amos (Amos 1:1)

7. Amos accused ___ of not keeping God's commands and laws. (Amos 2:4)

9. Amaziah, the ___ of Bethel, tried to chase Amos away. (Amos 7:10–13)

11. Amos told the people to hate what is ___. (Amos 5:15)

13. Amos accused the people of ___ of selling others into slavery. (Amos 1:6)

14. Amos compared the greedy women of Bashan to ___. (Amos 4:1)

17. Amos said the people hated those who told the ___. (Amos 5:10)

18. The Lord warned that the punishment of Israel would be so bad that people would run as if chased by a ___. (Amos 5:18–19)

DOWN

2. Occupation of Amos (Amos 1:1)

4. Amos said the rich of Israel ___ down the weak and poor. (Amos 2:7)

5. Amos had a vision of a basket of ___. (Amos 8:1–2)

8. Uzziah was ___ when Amos preached. (Amos 1:1)

10. The people of Israel were impatient for the ___ to end so that they could start selling and cheating again. (Amos 8:4–5)

12. The Lord sent Amos to prophesy to ___. (Amos 7:15)

15. Amos said the Lord wanted them to ___ singing in prayer because it was phony. (Amos 5:23)

16. Amos told the people to ___ what is right or good. (Amos 5:15)

83

Amos

Amos was a prophet in Israel during a time when that kingdom enjoyed considerable wealth. You might think that such good times would lead the people to worship God and follow the covenant in gratitude, but actually the opposite happened. Some people still worshipped false gods. Others went through the motions of worshipping God, but then failed to keep the covenant commandment to love their neighbors, especially those who were poor and helpless. Some even took advantage of poor people for their own gain.

Amos lived in the eighth century BC and described himself as a shepherd and tree trimmer. He was originally from the southern kingdom of Judah, but God sent him to be a prophet in the northern kingdom of Israel. Amos started out his message by condemning all the nations surrounding Israel, beginning with Gaza and ending with Judah. His audience must have enjoyed hearing all those other people condemned. But Amos saved his greatest condemnation for Israel, predicting that God would allow it to be destroyed because of its people's unfaithfulness. He also taught that God would not completely abandon his people; a few people would survive to carry on God's plan.

REFLECTION

Answer these questions after you have read about Amos.

1. Prophets like Amos give hope to those who are suffering unjustly. They tell people who are living ungodly lives to change their ways. Look at the news in the newspaper, on television, or online. Where in our world, or even in your city, would a prophet want to give hope, and where would he or she say, "Shape up!"?

2. In Amos 6:14 the prophet says that he is not a professional prophet. In fact, he is a shepherd and a person who takes care of fig trees. Because he is from Judah, he has to leave his job to come and be a prophet in Israel. Think of the types of careers you have thought about for yourself. How can one or more of these careers include the role of the prophet?

Bible Passages about Amos

Amos 2:4–8
Amos predicts God's judgment against Judah and Israel.

Amos 5:1–7
Amos calls people to turn away from false gods.

Amos 6:3–8
Amos's special warning to complacent rich people

Amos 7:1–9
Amos's visions from God

Amos 8:4–14
Amos condemns unjust practices.

Amos 9:11–15
Amos predicts a future restoration of Israel.

Breakthrough! Articles

Read these articles to learn more about Amos.

Breakthrough! Interview with Amos

Introduction to the Book of Amos